Glove Letters:

A Father Recalls
His Son's Greatest Game

Glove Letters:

A Father Recalls
His Son's Greatest Game

TAYLOR WILSON

The HillHelen
Group Publishers LLC

High praise for *Glove Letters*

"I was attached to Landon and his mission the day his dad shared his unique story with me. What a wonderful spirit this young man has for life, for people, for challenges, and the game of baseball. Taylor is kind enough to share his son's wonderful passion and perseverance with us all. I love this young man and his journey."

—Tim Corbin, head baseball coach, Vanderbilt University

"This story catches your emotions and pulls on your heart strings. Landon's narrative, written in letters from his dad, is remarkable."

—Bill Dance, fishing icon

"The beautiful game of baseball is many different things to many different people. For some, it's a vehicle for release, for others it's a means to an end, while some just simply love playing it. Some love coaching it and impacting kids through the life lessons woven into it. From the six-year-old playing T-ball to the MLB all-star, baseball simply provides 'something' magical and unpredictable . . . the anticipation of the next pitch. For Landon Wilson, baseball became ALL OF THE ABOVE. This is very eloquently described by his father, Taylor Wilson, in *Glove Letters*—a collection of letters from a dad to a son facing the difficulties caused by a severe accident. Landon's love for baseball, nurtured through the rehabilitation process and loving relationship between a father and his son, creates the epic true story of the champion of the comeback."

—Daron Schoenrock, head baseball coach,
The University of Memphis

"If I can do it . . . Landon, you can do it! With creativity, belief, and determination you will find that there isn't anything in this world you can't do. Just keep believing that . . . keep believing you are up for the challenge!"

—Jim Abbott, MLB pitcher

Library of Congress

ISBN: 978-1-7361525-6-0

Printed and bound in the United States of America
by Ingram Lightning Source

Editor's Note: The author chose to capitalize certain words
for emphasis.

Cover design by Gregg Bender;
special thanks to Oscar Esquivias for the cover photo

Editing, layout, and design:
Jacque Hillman, Kim Stewart, and Katie Gould

The HillHelen Group LLC
www.hillhelengrouppublishers.com
hillhelengroup@gmail.com

Dedication

For Beth and Landon.
Thanks for letting me be on your home team.
Glove, always.

Acknowledgments

Special thanks to God, family, friends,
first responders, medical personnel, and anyone offering
prayers and encouragement.
Also, I am grateful for my accountability team:
Pamela Dance, Daniel Mires,
Lynn (Col.) Sanders, and Allen Watts.
They made sure I kept writing
in the summer of '21 (even when they knew
I really wanted to be fishing).

Table of Contents

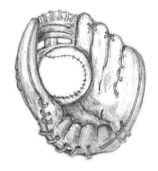

Introduction

A week after his eighteenth birthday, Landon Wilson was struck by a car while training for his senior year of baseball. He lost his arm and nearly his leg. He spent nearly fifty days in Regional One Health Medical Center in Memphis, Tennessee, undergoing eight surgeries. His is a tale of an epic battle to climb back on the pitching mound within months.

"Some aim to climb Mount Everest. My son's goal is to climb back atop a pitching mound," Landon's dad, Taylor Wilson, told a reporter after the accident.

A pitcher's mound is less than a foot higher than home plate; Everest is nearly 5.5 miles up. The mound isn't in the clouds like Everest, but in Landon's condition, it might as well have been. Still, his vision was clear and his goal admirable.

The question at the time: Was such a feat possible?

Several athletes have played baseball with one arm, but most were born with the challenge or had years to develop their talent. Fewer among their ranks are those who taught themselves how in five months, with one arm and literally one healthy leg to stand on.

Landon's injuries were many. In addition to a lost arm, he had a broken ankle with screws in one leg, and the other leg wasn't just broken. It had bone loss and a gaping wound, and it required titanium rods.

But his goal was focused.

Upon being told of the imminent removal of what was left of his arm, Landon Wilson told the ER surgeons at Elvis Presley Trauma Center:

"Just leave enough for me to hold a glove."

With baseball as a backdrop, this collection of letters from Wilson's dad is a study in Life's Game Plan and the faith, prayer, family, friends, willpower, and grace that miraculously got the youngster back atop the pitcher's mound.

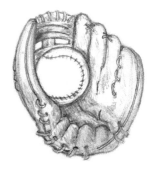

Prologue

D oes anyone write letters anymore?

Maybe social media has found a way to carry out some semblance of the tradition. And I suppose there is a World Wide Web of people out there participating in various forms of written communication.

But are social media posts, blips, and clips really *letters* in the old-fashioned sense?

Most likely, not.

Largely, old-school letter writing is gone. And it's a shame, too. Have you ever seen our predecessors' handwriting? It was art, be it calligraphy or cave paintings. Today, we creatively text works of art like: "TL;DR" (too long; didn't read), and honestly, the *L* should likely stand for lazy.

A self-professed man of letters, I like the handwriting idea. It takes my mind to something my old friend and former sports editor Dan Morris once told me after he interviewed the legendary basketball coach John Wooden.

Wooden lost his wife and for years afterward wrote monthly love letters to her and bundled them on the bed the two had shared. The story sounds almost too good to be true, but it is. Dan told me he saw the letters.

From all accounts, Wooden was inspirational. He said so many wonderful things while coaching. Speaking of love letters, he said, "Passion is temporary. Love is enduring."

Maybe that will be the case with the notes in this book. Love will endure.

Coach Wooden also reportedly said, "Things turn out best for people who make the best of the way things turn out."

Some of us know this truth in our heart. Some of us prove it.

Have I second-guessed telling the tale? Well, yes, and I have considered whether the story is as miraculous to me as it is to others. I am a dad, and a baseball dad at that, writing of his son, right? We humans love to brag on our children and our hunting dogs.

"Never brag on your dog before the hunt" is a saying for a reason. And then, too, as Dizzy Dean is claimed to have said, "It ain't bragging if it's the truth."

Oh, a dad talking about his boy, yes, some could put the whole thing in a fish-tale category. And with more than thirty years as an outdoor writer, well, I know something about those, too.

In contrast, this is a true story. (Wait a minute, that's how fish tales start, right?)

Maybe a question is, why undertake this in a series of letters? Well, I have long been more columnist than novelist, more sprinter than marathon man.

My initial thoughts are that letters are more personal. It's been said, "Letters are that which is often whispered in the corner to a friend." Letters are heartfelt, and specifically special in intent.

Typically, there are times in the lives of parents and children when they don't talk as much. Maybe it's Nature's way of assuring some degree of independence for both.

Also, letters might lend me another option to my son's ears, and maybe even his courageous heart.

I hope this letter format gives Landon a record and better understanding of his storm of a story. And maybe others will also catch some of the mystery and mojo, and even tie together the seams that make us believe in miracles. Maybe some will believe in the power of prayer.

A letter is basically storytelling, and I am certain from primitive fireside tales of the hunt and cave drawings onward, we humans have done our best to pass along tales of the day's wins or losses.

Of course, I am a storyteller. I come from a long line of them. And this story is mine, and told from my perspective, so there are things I can't tell, because I don't know. Maybe one day Landon will tell his version.

With each perspective, there is basically a different story. How great is that?

And stories are often lessons and legacies. For example: "Did I ever tell you how my grandmother made cornbread?" If her lesson is taught, her tale, even for something as simple as cornbread, continues.

You may remember the movie *Troy*. Achilles's mother tells him if he stays home, he will live a contented life with many generations to follow. If he goes to war, he will meet death, but they will tell his story forever.

Achilles chose to become a tale that lingers.

Many cultures see the honor of lingering in stories told. It's why I am writing these letters, to honor all that happened and its ingredients: perseverance, prayer, friends, family, love, etc.

And heck, what's the use of playing the Game of Life if there is no box score and the chance that our name might just be included in it?

Oh, most of us are more Archibald Wright "Moonlight" Graham than Babe Ruth, Hank Aaron, or my favorite, Stan "The Man" Musial.

Graham was celebrated in W. P. Kinsella's novel, *Shoeless Joe*, which became one of my favorite movies, *Field of Dreams*. By the way, Graham spent some minor league time in my West Tennessee region, playing for the Memphis Egyptians.

But in the majors, he only played one inning, with no contributions in the field or at the plate, in a blip of an appearance on the MLB radar in 1905. But as his character noted in the movie, "One inning can change the world." So maybe it's this shared communication, the telling of the tale of Landon Wilson's blip on the radar, however it's told, that I believe justifies a spot in Life's lineup.

Do we all have that potential for Andy Warhol's fifteen minutes of fame? Do we all have a Rudy Ruettiger moment on that Notre Dame field?

We all have a story, but do they all have merit?

This baseball dad thinks so. In the end, readers will be the judge.

Also, perhaps such tales are needed as life lessons, as primal proof of existence and survival?

For example, somebody had to return to the fire to tell how

he survived the saber-toothed tiger by using a pointed stick, right? And didn't somebody have to spin the first story about the acquisition of fire? And a wagon didn't have a wheel until someone shared the idea through a story.

As a teacher, I think all stories are teaching moments. By the way, Jesus, one of the greatest teachers I know, taught with parables.

I believe Landon's story was a game well played, and worth the recollections, be it by box score, cave drawing, or letters from Dad.

　　　　　　　　　　　　　　— *Taylor Wilson, baseball dad*

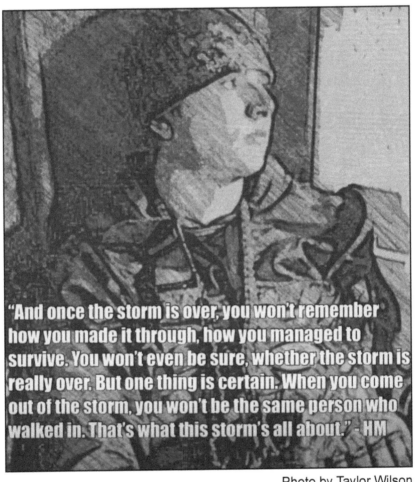

"And once the storm is over, you won't remember how you made it through, how you managed to survive. You won't even be sure, whether the storm is really over. But one thing is certain. When you come out of the storm, you won't be the same person who walked in. That's what this storm's all about." - HM

Photo by Taylor Wilson

Taylor Wilson often looks at this photo of his son, Landon Wilson, in a duck blind. On the photo, Taylor had placed an inspirational quote by Japanese author Haruki Murakami.

"Hello, darkness, my old friend,
I've come to talk to you again."

Paul Simon and Art Garfunkel,
"The Sound of Silence"

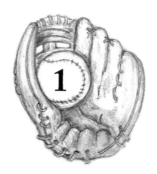

The Shadows in My Soul

Dear Landon,

I have lingered and lamented this specific letter because it compels me to go somewhere very dark in my mind's eye. And honestly, it's somewhere that's never far away. Once awakened, it's a memory I sense is dangerous for me to hold close.

But if you'll bear with me, I know I'll come out of it simply because I know what the late Paul Harvey called *the rest of the story.*

Like that old weekly episode of a TV Western, you kind of know the hero is going to make it, because the show must go on.

I also make it back to the light because I have the gifts of God, a strong prayer group, family, friends, and a son who had evidently not only listened but believed that Engine-That-Could story he heard as a kid.

* * *

Sitting on the porch, I looked at the fading and late October sun falling over my neighbor's silo. In our part of the world, October is the best time for photography because of the unique light, a result of the seasonal tilt of the earth. Afternoons are silhouetted with an apt amount of black and orange, the colors of impending Halloween.

And with our planet tilted just so, fall was upon us, my favorite time of the year. Little did I know, it would soon seem our family was about to fall off into deep space.

* * *

A lot of people believe pitching to be all about arms. They're wrong. Pitching also has much to do with the legs.

Following an impressive summer of club ball, you were getting some interest from several small colleges. Advice from sound sources said with your six-foot-six-inch frame and increased velocity, better scholarship opportunities would present themselves, especially with a strong senior year. So, to strengthen your legs, you had begun a running regimen and were doing well with it.

I would later ask God why you should receive such a life-changing setback, while basically doing something to make yourself better. I suspect He answered that irony later in your story. Your opinion may differ.

But that night, as I sat on our front steps, you and I disagreed about the route. I suggested going to town, and you said you'd run from home.

This is not an I-told-you-so deal, at all. I hold myself very accountable for letting you go, and I probably always will. Later, at night in the hospital, I would dream of standing up from my sleep and hear myself shouting, "Don't go!"

I even remember thinking that twilight was the time of most accidents. And in my mind, I knew how dangerous our road, with no shoulders and deepening ditches, was and is.

How I would later wish I had gotten into a big fight with you about that. Maybe minutes of arguing would have been all it took to throw off the timing of what happened.

I looked at your mom. She went inside and got you wearable reflectors and made you put them on.

But off you went. "Thus began our longest journey," as Scout says in *To Kill a Mockingbird*.

I began preparing supper. It was spaghetti, which, by the way, I have never cooked again. Have you ever eaten something and got sick, and never really wanted to eat it again? Preparing spaghetti is like that with me now.

An opened envelope with your ACT score of 29 was on our kitchen's island. It was one mere point away from reaching the famed 30 that everyone knows means more scholarship money. Regardless, a 29 was something of which to be proud.

The envelope and the spaghetti would still be there when I returned weeks later to check quickly on our home.

Time went by. You'd been gone awhile. Darkness fell. At one point, I heard a strange and unique whirring noise; it's something else that would later haunt my dreams.

Eventually, I went out on the porch, and there were blue lights on the hill to the south. I ran for your mom and yelled something I don't remember.

We got in my truck. I stomped it through the drive and told your mom, "START PRAYING, NOW!"

We arrived on the hill less than a half-mile from our home. Approaching the group of first responders, I walked by a small truck pulling a trailer, parked alongside the road. I remember running my hand along the front of it (it was the side that first struck you) and thinking how unusually cold it seemed. The lights were off. It was hooked to a trailer, which I now know had to likewise do damage to your body.

Today, I still have an aversion to working with a similar trailer I own, especially if I allow my mind time to wander.

An officer who met me said something about the road being

blocked. Your mom talked to him, and I remember him saying, "This is the kid's parents."

My heart fell from a height that it would never achieve again.

I walked into a well-lit area. For such a dark situation, there sure was a lot of light. I can still see everything in my memory.

We were all encircled in brightness, with black night all around the edges. In the light, people were working. When my mind muses that moment, it seems the horror is fended off by the fight for humanity. I knew a pack of people were waging a war to help you.

I don't think I read the faces of anyone there, maybe because I thought I might read too much in their eyes. I did not know if you were alive.

My stepbrother David Scott, a law enforcement officer, was there. How thankful am I that he, someone you knew well, had already reached you. It's a salve of sorts to know you were comforted at such a time.

Later, I would also learn that our neighbor Carrie McCage had rushed down to you, since you were close to her home, basically fallen in her yard.

Obviously in shock, you told her that if she could help you up, you could make it home. You said this with literally no leg to stand on at the time. I think it was also Carrie who would retrieve the reflectors your mom made you wear, along with your shoes and a crushed, padded headset that may very well have prevented brain damage.

It was David who escorted me to your body.

I instantly saw you were alive, and then my eyes wandered to gauge the scene. My relief reeled when I saw your body. Your left arm was hanging on by a thread, and your right leg was not where it was supposed to be.

I turned and stuck my entire torso in through the open window of my old pickup. It was the same truck where, as a child, you got down in the floorboard to hide your own tears upon learning of your uncle's death. That same uncle was air-lifted mere yards from the same spot you were about to be given flight.

I felt the need to hide my pain, too.

David followed me and put his hand on my shoulder. I returned to the now, nearly lost in heartbreak.

It was like that moment in a boxing match where the announcer notes a near knockout.

"Boy, Wilson got lucky to stay on his feet that time," the late broadcaster Howard Cosell might say in his blustery voice.

I staggered all right, but my thoughts of you and your mother went like this: "I can't lose it. I've got to be here, in the *now*." I returned to where you'd fallen, wanting you to see me, wanting you to know I was there.

Here, you probably think of your old man as a wimp. That's OK, I have long admitted being the weak link in the chain. My only defense for my weakness is the immeasurable flood of emotions that capture the soul when one's child has been severely hurt.

In contrast, your mom's calmness and control were comforting. She talked to you as if nothing were wrong, in a voice certain all was going to be well, even though on the edges of that light wrapped 'round us, my own ears were fending off the whirling wails of chaos.

She was constant in the crazy; it kept me tethered and grounded.

Your mom is walking, talking, praying, real-life proof of the oh-so-powerful abstract trinity of faith, hope, and love. And on that night, she instantly transformed into an anchor of hope that could hold steady a fleet of *Titanics* in a hurricane.

She talked to you with a shared certainty that all *would* be well. This attribute would surface again and again, especially when she talked to your doctors.

Looking at you, I remember you saying, "This is all so surreal."

You also told the crew around you to check on the driver who hit you.

"Y'all need to check on him, I want to make sure he's all right," you said.

That, too, was incredible poise and maturity for someone whose battered body had just turned eighteen.

Was it the trauma or drugs they may have already given you talking? I don't know, but I still admire you so for those few lines.

We would later learn details about the driver. As of this writing, none of us has spoken with him since.

Someone told us they were taking you to downtown Memphis and the Elvis Presley Trauma Center, which is part of what West Tennesseans still call The Med. We were to follow in our vehicle.

Now, it seems as if only you, your mom, and I stood there at that moment. I remember you looking at your mom and me, and saying, "He can't drive." Obviously, you had your wits about you even in the shock. I was a wreck waiting to happen, which, when I think about it, has probably always been a metaphor for my life.

I've been blessed with so many people who have helped keep me on track.

When I was alone with your mom, my quick, mumbled assessment was that you would live. But I knew your arm and likely the leg were gone. I didn't say it, but I also knew the center ring on your life's target, baseball, was also gone forever.

Well, so thought doubting Thomas, or in this case, doubting Taylor. But God and you had other plans that you would let us all in on later.

For months, I had been praying to calm a gut feeling that something bad was going to happen.

Well, it had arrived, and God came with it.

I've meditated that moment many times. I have pondered if my prayers made a difference or was it a waste? The answer that comes to my mind is that *prayers always make a difference.*

My faith says God is everywhere. But in reflection, He was notably there that night. He had to be. He gave your mom and me untold strength in a moment when it seemed the earth had opened to hell, and we were all going in The Pit that poet William Ernest Henley mentions in "Invictus." (More on the poem later.)

Sure, in the time ahead, we would continue to waver along the edges, but we wouldn't fall in.

A first responder later told your mother that they had never seen relatives handle the scene of such a serious accident as calmly as we did. More than likely, I was just shocked into numbness.

Before you lifted off, you told the crew you had just made a 29 on your ACT, and that you were going to make a 30 the next time around. That never happened, but you would happen to do some other stuff, which to me was even more impressive.

I don't remember much about the trip to Memphis, other than being glad you would be there a long time ahead of us.

"I want to cry, but I just can't," I told Beth.

She, the rock, carried on conversation as normal as it could be, maintained control, and got us there.

We arrived at the downtown Trauma Center, what I later would call Ground Zero. It was the famed belly of the beast. In a nightmarish haze, I pondered if it would swallow us all.

Friends and family had also arrived. We weren't fighting alone, thank God. But it was all or nothing at that point, and I will tell you this. I could not have picked a better team to fight with: you, your mom, family, friends, God, and what we would discover later was an army of prayer warriors from our town and from all over the country.

* * *

At the heart of it, Landon, this letter is about knowing of the metaphorical darkness in the world—knowing, understanding, surviving it. The key is likewise recognizing the presence of emblematic light.

Of course, knowing a light is out there combatting darkness in the world is one thing. Seeing it is another.

There's an old story about Grand Ole Opry comic and country star Minnie Pearl and a promoter driving Hank Williams around in a car. They were trying to get the wasted and talented singer to where he could perform. They were trying a singalong of Williams's "I Saw the Light," and he stopped and told her, "I don't see no light. There ain't no light."

Lord knows, as a dad with a son so injured, I was there, too. Looking for light and any trace of it. But we made it through what "Invictus" poet Henley called the "fell clutch of circumstance" and "bludgeonings of chance."

I hope the darkness I speak of in this letter never finds you. I wish I could promise you that you would always be bathed in light, but Life doesn't work like that.

As they say, storms are always there. Tempests are always approaching. Either one's passing, approaching, or you're in the middle of it.

I have a photo of you in a duck blind. You're gazing into the distance. On the photo, I placed a quote by Japanese author Haruki Murakami. His words are: "And once the storm is over, you won't remember how you made it through, how you managed to survive. You won't even be sure whether the storm is really over. But one thing is certain. When you come out of the storm, you won't be the same person who walked in. That's what this storm's all about."

The key to surviving troubled waters is also to have the right crew in the boat. Our family did survive this storm. We did see the light, through its darkest journey, all through what I always recognize again, again, and again: God, prayer, family, friends, and an engine that could and will.

Photo by Oscar Esquivias

Landon and his high school teammates gather in a prayer circle before a game.

"Most people want to be circled by safety, not by the unexpected. The unexpected can take you out. But the unexpected can also take over and change your life."

Denver Moore, co-author, *Same Kind of Different as Me*

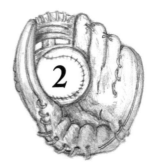

Baseball, Hope, Circles, Souls

Dear Landon,

I've never told you this, but I have prayed for you daily since you made our Team Wilson's lineup. And trust me, that circle of prayer is still unbroken.

You arrived a month earlier than expected on this round world, traveling with other round planets, all in like circles, around a life-giving ball of gas, which some scientists have come to claim is the most perfect sphere in the universe.

You could cue Elton John's "Circle of Life" here if you want, and yes, I may already have made you dizzy.

Sorry, but I am not stopping there.

Think about a baseball. It's a concentric circle, made up of circles: wool, poly/cotton windings surround a round cork pill.

Of course, our existence is likewise surrounded with rounds. Onions, onion rings, rings within the trunks of trees, and ripples in ponds are all concentric circles. They're everywhere!

In that regard, there's much irony in that a zero can mean nothing, but a circle can signify nearly everything.

In my faith, we are always simply rounding the bases, heading Home. Round and round.

"So, in a way, we are all homeless—just working our way home," said the homeless man who changed the world in *Same Kind of Different as Me.*

We're all making that big circle, and in a world of spheres, baseball is likely the one most dear to your heart.

I am partly to blame for your love of the Game, but others helped. Your grandfather, other relatives, coaches, and friends all helped you become spellbound to the diamond.

As with my daily prayers, I also sometimes held you and sang you to sleep at night. Talk about scary? The playlist was short, with you sometimes getting a reprieve via a CD of old 1970s soul songs. I hope you one day go back and rediscover such cradle music. Percy Sledge will be a good place to start.

In your nursery, "Take Me Out to the Ballgame" was the nocturnal solo I butchered the most, there in the dark with a nightlight filled with bubbling plastic fish. Of course, I plugged into the lyrics, "root, root, root for *the Cardinals,*" instead of the traditional *"home team."* We come from generations of Cardinals fans, so that was a given. As John Grisham noted in the novel *A Painted House,* many of us flatlanders on both sides of the Mississippi River's Delta were indoctrinated into the Cardinal red religion via old-time radio broadcasts from far to the north in St. Louis.

Oh, there were defectors with the advent of cable Turner Broadcast System and Ted Turner's Braves, and of course much, much worse, WGN's Chicago Cubs. But we Wilsons remained loyal to the Birds on the Bat.

But back to lullabies. Perhaps, a time or two maybe, I might have been in the same zip code as what's called *in key,* but I doubt it.

In reflection, those new to fatherhood do strange things. Hopefully, I instilled a love for baseball and music. Both are wins.

And here's where I'd be lying to you if I didn't confess to singing "Somewhere Over the Rainbow."

A recording of *Taylor Wilson, LIVE Lullabies* would be a cool thing for me to have now. How much would your old man pay for that memory? Lots. But rest assured, I'd be the only one to enjoy it.

As for "Rainbow," I'll admit, it's not the manliest of tunes, and I am far from Judy Garland. My version was (at quite the stretch) more along the lines of Jerry Lee Lewis or Israel "IZ" Kamakawiwo'ole. Check those out. Maybe you ought to check Jerry Lee's first. After all, your preschool music teacher did tell me you told her you were The Killer once, after kicking over the bench to her piano. Another admitted she'd never had a grade school student show up with a Cardinal red Mohawk and a KISS T-shirt, either.

But as for "Rainbow," hey, in my defense, it's a song of hope.

So again, fresh to the world, I was teaching you hope and baseball, mixed with some rock, some soul. How could you go wrong?

Hope, of the famed trilogy hope, faith, and love, carries the most weight and springs eternal, as they say, with each season of our lives. And new baseball seasons have always stirred hope, even for the worst of teams.

My thoughts, hopes, and prayers have always been geared toward helping you one day round third and make it toward the Home that Denver Moore mentioned.

But then came the day my compulsion to pray for you became as urgent as that last out needed for a Series win.

In the months before your accident, I had this foreboding concern not just for you, but for those around me. It was a dark, never-ending inkling, like an exasperating itch, in the middle of my back, that I couldn't reach.

I sat in the driveway daily before I left for work and said,

"Lord, protect my family and my friends. Bless and keep them and help them find their way to you." And I mean I did this for months, seemingly out of the blue. Not a bad thing, mind you, but it became something of a chant to scare off a dark blotch that I could feel more than see.

Still, prayers or not . . . the accident happened, which was highlighted by a helicopter trip, nearly fifty days in Regional Medical Center, in Memphis, and you with an amputated left arm, broken bones in both legs, and a hell of a mountain to climb.

But you were alive.

I still remember being dazed in the darkness of a waiting room and covered in a heartache of fog and an abrasive, blue blanket.

Then, this voice said, "Taylor, he's alive."

It was said in a comforting tone, and to this day, I swear it was the voice of my late uncle, Ronnie Taylor. He gave me his time when I was young. He took me hunting, and I am forever grateful.

I picked you up from preschool the day he died, and, embarrassed, you asked if you could hide in the floorboard and cry. I remember being a bit ashamed of the fact that I'd taught you to hide honest emotions.

Today, I am at an age where I regret not having displayed my most honest tears and emotions.

The helicopter that took you to Memphis had years prior landed in nearly the same spot to carry my injured uncle to the ER. His earthly story was ending with his flight; yours was only beginning.

I was turkey hunting when his helicopter passed overhead. I didn't know who it was, but I remember taking a knee in prayer and looking up at the belly of the chopper. Talk about prayer circles.

But let's return to "He's alive." I opened my eyes to see the soothing voice, and it was my cousin Randall, Ronnie's eldest. I'll swear to this day he delivered a message from his father, whether Randall knows it or not.

Of course, as a Christian, the Biblical words "He's alive" have always had weight with me—and it's not a bad Dolly Parton song, either. But how I have since endured on these words and marveled that they were delivered to me in a time of great darkness.

Those same words have helped me fend off sudden anxiety when I approach daily the location where you were struck.

You were alive, and emergency-room hours later, you were stitched up, reassembled to begin what would be your best game ever. But that could be debated. I have long since learned not to doubt anything when it comes to you . . . or prayers.

* * *

There are 108 double stitches in a baseball, a purity of white leather held together by blood red seams. You'd better believe, as a Christian, I see a metaphor there.

Before a baseball can be used in a Major League game, it must be rubbed and smudged up a bit to be held better, take the sheen off, and help grip the ball. All this Big League, perfect, baseball-rubbing mud comes from the New Jersey side of the Delaware River and complies with MLB Rule 4.01(c).

I don't know if you remember or not, but we once stood above the bullpen at Busch Stadium and watched a player and coach complete this pregame ritual. My mind's eye recalls it as pitching coach Dave Duncan and Yadier Molina, but it's hard to believe they stooped to the menial tasks.

In musings of all you went through, I sometimes kind of like to rationalize it as Life put some mud on you to make you better for the Game.

It's a positive way to look at it, and I may see it that way entirely for selfish reasons. It helps me cope with what happened to you. But there could be something deeper there. I mean God scooped up some soil and created us, right?

Dust to dust; Delaware rubbing mud to mud?

Regardless, you now know a little about being scuffed. I remember standing beside you in ICU at Regional Medical Center when a brawny and bearded nurse, with an obviously kind heart (what good nurse doesn't have one?), kneeled beside you and said: "Landon, tell me. I just *must* know . . . you have no spinal injuries, no brain injuries, no internal injuries. After all your body went through, how on Earth did this happen? There has to be a reason you are still here!"

In classic Landon Wilson style, you replied, "Oh, I am here for a reason. I just have to figure out what it is."

I remember seeing a faraway look in your blue-green eyes when you replied. All the while, I stood there, pondering hope, a hope that a lot of folks were rooting for the home team, 'cause if we were pulling off a win, we'd need prayers, a mountain of them.

Little did we know this mountain of prayers would bolster an unimaginable will, already ignited in the emergency room. That's where you had plainly told the surgeons your plan.

When they said the removal of your left arm was imminent, you simply replied, "Just leave enough for me to hold my glove."

Few leave this world without being roughed up. I guess the best we can expect is that our seams hold tight as we're tossed and knocked around. Of course, having the heart of a lion doesn't hurt one's cause, either.

Photo by April Gentry

Landon pitches his last game before the accident. He struck out eleven in a win for his Batters Box club team.

"Do not boast about tomorrow,
for you do not know what a day may bring."

Proverbs 27:1

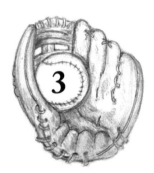

Showing Promise

Dear Landon,

Even before the accident, you were not the typical flame-thrower. You were the thinking pitcher who methodically got outs or opportunities for outs. Like a hitter's ability to consistently get on base, a pitcher's ability to simply get outs is an overlooked talent that leans toward more wins.

As Hall of Famer Sandy Koufax noted, a pitcher becomes better when he strives more toward making a batter hit the ball than on making them miss.

And, too, there's that famed line from Crash Davis in *Bull Durham*: "Strikeouts are boring. Besides that, they're fascist."

Before your injury, you were increasingly becoming better. It was an exciting time of possibility and promise. Great expectations heralded your senior year. The summer before the accident, you pitched and played extremely well on your club team that traveled the Southeast.

The last game you pitched (fully abled as they say), late summer before your accident, saw you tossing a win against an older and more experienced JUCO team. It was a doubleheader, and you won the game you pitched with eleven strikeouts.

If I had to pick and carry a memory of the last game I pitched with two arms, that would be a good one to haul around.

Your slider was dangerous that day.

Promise was on the horizon. Throw in your big, tall frame and add increased velocity, which was coming with the leg training, and who knows? You likely could have had a solid college career. Perhaps at a JUCO or a mid-sized school. Maybe more. The interest was there.

Life was good. And then it wasn't. It happens. I believe the Grand Design must be so. It must be cyclic. Highs, lows, and in-betweens. Round and round we go, with constant agitation keeping us from becoming stagnant.

The reason we relate to stories is conflict. No conflict, no story. In baseball, the pitcher (part athlete, part actor, part magician) is in the middle of the conflict, in a game loaded with frustration and failure.

The hero or heroine of a story must suffer, regardless of the win or loss. To get better, he or she must be tested.

To know that is probably better than to linger too long on the past. What-ifs are worthless as warm water through those ballpark fountains from which no one really should drink. And to tell the truth, they often leave the same taste in your mouth.

We live and die in the now. It's all we have.

Memories of the past and possibilities of the future can be good, but the moment we're in is really all we have.

As a pitcher, you know this better than most.

You can't worry about the pitch before or after. The only pitch you must work with is the one you have in your hand right now. This philosophy is straight out of the playbook of Harvey A.

Dorfman, a mental skills coach who wrote *The Mental ABC's of Pitching* and was a pioneer in sports psychology.

So, hero, what are you going to toss at Life, especially in those times when it is ready to beat you down with a Louisville Slugger?

That, youngster, is up to you. But Dad being Dad, I am sitting on it being a slider.

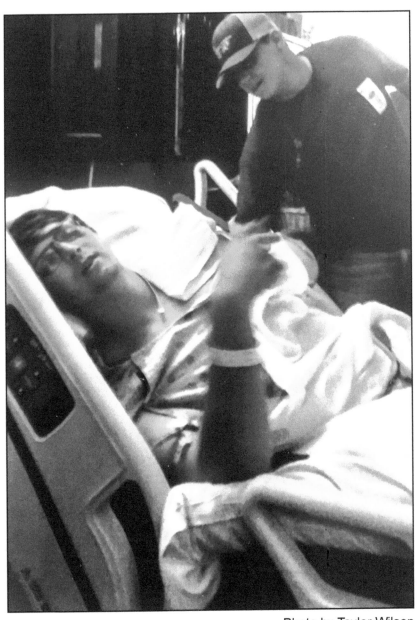

Photo by Taylor Wilson

Many of Landon's teammates from various teams showed up
after the accident to let Landon know that they had his back.
Bandits teammate Collin Fletcher even scratched his back!

> *"You spend a good piece of your life gripping a baseball, and in the end, it turns out it was the other way around all the time."*
>
> Jim Bouton, MLB pitcher, author of *Ball Four*

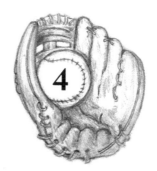

Have Bat, Did Travel

Dear Landon,

You are a product of the travel ball system.

Folks typically love it or hate it.

The bad? Well, the short list is costs, the damage it has done to community league participation, parental craziness, and a kid having too many eggs in one basket.

The good, of course, is the lessons learned, the love and respect for the game, and the friendships and memories made.

But all these pros and cons could be said about any large-scale activity children become involved in.

Does it burn kids out? Well, yeah, but it also creates some baseball-playing machines.

People often carefully questioned your mom and me (and maybe even eyed us somewhat suspiciously) about your participation in travel ball.

It is a subculture. You travel all over the place with the same families and become diamond gypsies for much of the year. Again, the same thing could be said of all the other youth activities.

Our thoughts were this: Our kid loves it, so let's go all in. If he stops loving it, well, we will move on to the next thing.

You never stopped loving it.

Of course, there is the parental push for success and the phrase "taking it to the next level." I don't think we took it that far. An interest in playing in college was building at the time you got hurt. But I was never ignorant of how incredibly hard it is to make it to the upper ranks of the baseball world.

Again, we wanted you to play for as long as you wanted because you loved the game.

I think you did just that.

The National Collegiate Athletic Association has recognized in an advertisement that less than 2 percent of its student athletes go pro, stressing instead the value of their degrees.

An extremely low percentage of all of history's minor league players have made it to the big leagues.

This is the case with all sports. The pyramid for it has numbers of youth league players, then rises and narrows to school level, narrower at college, even more so for minors, and extraordinarily little room at the top for pros.

I've even drawn the same graphic as a funnel on the board at school to represent the same concept.

"Now, Mr. Wilson isn't telling anyone to give up your dreams. I just won't do that. But after looking at this graphic, we can kind of see how it's smart to have a famed Plan B, C, and maybe D and E. And learning all you can in school helps with all letters of the plan," I tell them.

Most often, they roll their eyes, and sneak looks at their mobile phones hidden in their laps.

One more hurdle to the "next level" is natural—genetics.

Some have the athletic genes, some don't. And few have the pro gene. We may all have the dreams, but we don't all have the genes.

I even think finding success in your trial was linked to genetics. As I've noted, thank goodness you take after your mom, especially in the stubborn, won't-give-up part.

There is absolutely nothing wrong with being the best player you can be, at whatever the level.

We were into travel ball because you loved the game.

I played a version of travel ball once. It was way back in the day, and most of the team piled into Coach Greg Vanstory's 1960-something car, with a window knocked out from a stray foul ball. We went to far-off communities, most within a thirty-minute drive, but the world was smaller then.

Oh, it was primitive in comparison to travel ball today. But I will tell you this—my friends on that team are my friends today. I don't see them much, but if I had just sent out a lifeline from the middle of the Mississippi River, most would be wet already trying to get here, right now, to help—even if it's upstream.

No one can buy those memories from me, or that type of friend.

By the way, I saw one of your travel ball buds come into that hospital and scratch a teammate's back, because his teammate had lost an arm and couldn't reach the itch. Do you get the picture? It's powerful stuff in my scorebook.

Yes, the sweetest icing on that portion of cake was the friendships and memories you made. You saw proof of that when you were injured. Your travel ball families poured into that hospital right alongside all your other family and friends.

They showed up and showed how much they loved and supported you. Could anyone ask for more?

Oh, in the post-playing years of your life, you've found other things to occupy your time, golf among them. But you still love the game, and especially those you learned to love it with.

I told someone once, "What will happen with Landon and baseball? Well, it's like this. I want something that connects us forever. Now, there's already a list of those things, but baseball is one of them. In my head, I see an older me and middle-aged Landon, standing at that statue of Stan Musial at Busch Stadium in St. Louis, an annual pilgrimage of sorts. Whether grandkids are there is up to Landon. We don't have to say much; we just know things. And one of them is baseball has meant more than a game to us. We have both traveled its base paths, and it's a connection I am glad we share."

"Here stands baseball's perfect warrior . . .
here stands baseball's perfect knight."

Ford Frick, baseball commissioner,
inscription on Stan Musial statue at Busch Stadium

Photo by Taylor Wilson

We may all be told at some point that we can no longer play the children's game, but some of us, like Landon, refuse to believe it.

"We're all told at some point in time that we can no longer play the children's game. We just don't know when that's gonna be. Some of us are told at eighteen, some of us are told at forty, but we're all told."

Baseball scout, movie, *Moneyball*

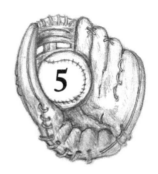

A Shelf Life for Our Seasons

Dear Landon,

As an old journalist, I have long been fascinated with quotes. Maybe it's because I spent roughly twenty-five years of my life sitting around waiting on someone to say something moving or entertaining. I define good writing as that which makes you think or feel, so in turn, a great quote writes a great story. But what do I know?

Also firmly established in my journalistic roots are the lessons of an old college professor:

1.) "Don't assume, because when you do, you make an ass out of *u* and (more importantly) *me*." He'd circle those letters on the board with zest, and make the chalk click on the board.

2.) "I don't care if your mom says she loves you; you'd better get me a second source." (That's because, see number one, "make an ass out of *u* and *me*.")

So, in my pursuit of truth in writing, I always backed it up with confirmatory quotes, which you may see throughout this book and in most of my conversations.

Now this quote, the "We are all told" at the beginning of this letter, has haunted me. Before your injury, even watching you play the Game, knowing one day it would end was always warming up in the bullpen of my mind. I guess it's a grownup thing.

As soon as our children arrive, many of us also begin to think of them leaving the nest.

As a one-time ballplayer, now relegated to the bleachers, and already likely headed into life's late innings, I know our seasons in the sun end. When you get old, like me, you only hope the memory banks have enough innings to get you through. One day, you just wake up and know to appreciate the smells of ballparks, cowhide, saddle soap (for conditioning gloves), and fresh clipped grass, and the sounds of an approving crowd and solid contact.

There's a recollection stuck in every former player's head. Maybe it's hitting a ball that still sails forever, making a play-of-the-day catch, or striking out the side. But just as we are all told, we all also keep such treasures hidden in our mind fields to help us make it through the inevitable bad days Life will dish up on a plate much bigger than the one ballplayers call home.

Knowing the certainty of "one day it will end," I watched you grow through T-ball, coach-pitch, and onward. As a parent and a former player, I did it with the sentiment of "Let's make the best memories we can." That was always part of the plan.

Of course, the maturity of knowing that things end can be a blessing or a curse. But "maybe time running out is a gift," as songwriter and Atlanta Braves fan Jason Isbell penned in his song, "If We Were Vampires."

The argument for life's time limits was also in the movie *Troy*. Achilles points out that the Greek gods envy us because humans enjoy things more, knowing every moment could be our last.

We all have that fast and firm shelf life.

But because things end, do we really appreciate them more? The logic says we should, but when we're young and bulletproof, we probably don't. We think the game goes on forever. We also get in our famed day-to-day ruts and forget to smell the infield's fresh-mowed grass, much less the metaphorical roses.

But there is also a blessing of being young and perhaps ignorant—not a bad word, by the way. There's nothing wrong with not knowing; one can always learn.

Youngsters heal faster, as you proved, and maybe, just maybe, youth sanctions you the luxury of ignoring the impossible.

It's as Guy and Susanna Clark wrote in "The Cape": "He did not know he could not fly, so he did."

And to add more evidence of affirmation, there's what Will Wilberforce said in *Amazing Grace*: "We are too young to realize that certain things are impossible . . . so we will do them anyway."

Is that how you did it? Did you make it back to the mound because you didn't know better? Maybe, but I suspect there was more in your miracle's gas tank.

And, of course, everything ends, and most often outside anyone's control. You could have died in that accident. As a parent, that's a horror far worse than the trepidation of watching you play your last game.

But timing is everything, and key, according to cliches. If what had happened to you had occurred in the time of the COVID-19 pandemic, the opportunity to get back to the game, post-injury and in your senior season, would have never been available.

I have often thought of the Perfect Storm you were caught in. I've considered how the bad things had to line up precisely for you to be injured, for you to be in that famed spot, and on that famed X marking the tragic results.

But there's another side of the scoreboard, too, for the positive fans among us. If so many good things—time and otherwise (first responders, doctors, procedures, therapy, coaches)—had not also fallen so seamlessly into place, you'd likewise never have reached your goal of once again climbing aloft the pitcher's mound.

It's a crazy question, and I ask a lot of them: *Does God use bad timing to make good things happen?*

I think He does it all the time. He constantly makes the impossible, possible.

Look at the sheer remoteness of known life in our universe and comprehend this.

Crazy question number 2: *What's time to God; does he even have to aggregate (count/tally/calculate)?*

My belief is simple enough for my simple mind: He speaks, and it happens.

I figure in your case, He said, "Play ball!" Heck, He may have even been specific: "Landon Wilson, play ball!"

Crazy question number 3: *Can you imagine your name being called by God?*

We can't argue it happened. I was a witness, there in the cheap seats. Yes, in reflection, God's stars aligned for you to get back on that mound. I call it a miracle, while others may call it luck.

We are ALL told we can no longer play the children's game.

Still, say it is so, Joe/Landon—sometimes, maybe a persevering soul may get a reprieve via decree from the Umpire in Chief.

I knew I'd one day watch your last game. What I didn't know was that you'd single-handedly (literally, in this case) select it . . . and defy the odds to play it.

Landon's pitching genes may well have come from his great-grandmother Mattie Belle Taylor, who was quite the character.

Photos courtesy of Taylor Wilson

"The hand that rocks the cradle indeed rules the world,
but it can also play ball."

Dad

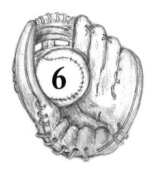

Grandma, Mamaw, and Gertie

Dear Landon,

To know where you are going, you need to know where you have been. And I tend to take it a step further. I think you also need to know who you come from. DNA can be potent and life-shaping.

Where'd you get your pitching arm and athletic abilities?

It wasn't from me—not directly, anyway.

In my mind's flight of fancy, I like to think some of it came from several of your family's matriarchs.

It may have been from your great-grandmother Mattie Belle Taylor. She was an amazing lady.

One of my favorite stories is how she was planting her garden and looked behind her to find an Ancona hen scratching up and eating her recently planted peas.

"I was so mad!" she told me. "I took a dirt clod and chunked it and hit that hen right in the head, killing it dead enough to flop a little. Then I grabbed it and went and got a butcher knife. I got my peas out its craw and replanted. We ate that hen for dinner," she laughed matter-of-factly at tale's end.

So there's one branch of the family tree with some pitching accuracy. How many folks can hit a hen in the head with a dirt clod?

Mattie Belle was also a talented basketball player, way back when she played basketball for her country community team. A solid family rumor was she once ran wild for the Providence Community basketball team, scoring over fifty points in one game.

Back in the day, the little communities that dotted counties had local sports teams, each with their own school. Many times when I was growing up, old folks would point at pastures or cotton fields in the middle of nowhere and say, "That's where we used to play ball."

My storyteller's imagination went wild when I looked on those fields, some with remnants of homemade backstops still standing.

Another family legend is that your great-great-aunt Sue secretly played for a men's team. She was found out only after she was knocked unconscious and had to be taken to the doctor.

I have a couple of photos of your great-grandmother, Mattie Belle, that I treasure. One is where she is riding a camel near a pyramid in the Holy Land, which was a long way from her West Tennessee cottonfield roots, and in another, she is holding an over-under shotgun with an I-know-how-to-use-this look on her face.

Your hitting may have come from your maternal grandmother.

When I was a kid, I'd stand for hours and hit things with a broom handle: black walnuts, rocks, and carpenter bees. The walnuts and rocks made feel-good sounds off the bat, but the bees were the most fun. They'd buzz the barn and tractor sheds, boring into the wood. I'd toss a rock up in the air and they'd follow it down into the strike zone.

You had to be extremely good to pull it off, but it was that homerun contact you felt when you managed to smack one that made you feel good all over. The bee? Well, not so much. And it's true others would cheat (with frustration) and get a tennis or badminton racket, but it was the broom handle that measured the skill of a master.

Once, I was reminiscing about carpenter-bee baseball when your maternal grandmother, Amy Deverell Hinsley, told me she also did that as a kid. I'd always thought I'd invented it, but realistically what were country kids to do back before phones and video games? When she told me, I immediately shared an unspoken and closer kinship with my mother-in-law.

"I think it made me a better hitter," I said.

Her eyes twinkled a little at her own memory.

"I always thought it did for me, too," she said.

Mrs. Amy played softball into her sixties.

Another matriarchal influence was your great-great-aunt Geraldine Williams, sister and polar opposite to Mattie Belle. Geraldine would literally dance well into her nineties before she gave up the ghost and went to a better and more elevated dance floor. She had to be in her late fifties when she took time to play baseball with me as a child. By the way, I am thinking she was closing in on eighty when she played ball with you.

As noted, there are a lot of influential seams that hold together who we are—what we become. And sometimes, when they say diamonds are a girl's best friend, they speak of those with bases on the corners.

Coach Buttermaker: [looks at Tanner's black eye]
What the hell happened to you, Tanner?

Engelberg: Tanner got into a fight. [because of the first game loss]

Coach Buttermaker: Who with?

Engelberg: The seventh grade.

Coach Buttermaker: What?

Engelberg: [shouts] The seventh grade!

The Bad News Bears, 1976

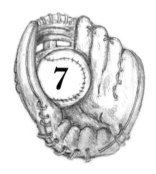

Tempered Stock

Dear Landon,

This collection of letters is not to bill anyone as perfect.
Not you, and especially not me.
You certainly know my faults, and I know yours.

In baseball, as a coach, I was tossed out of basically every level up to high school.

I am akin to the former Atlanta Braves coach Bobby Cox, who holds the Major League record at 161 times.

(I was the same way as a player.)

My favorite heave-ho as a coach was when an umpire kicked me out for something someone else had said. It really happened.

"You're outta here! I heard what you said," the ump said.

"Well, that's funny. Up until this point, I was just worried about your *eyesight*, but obviously you have *hearing* problems, too!" I replied.

Despite a good one-liner, I was gone for good on that one.

Yep, I have something I call the Taylor temper, that was handed down to me from generations on my mom's side. Throw in a dose of smart-ass (which probably just developed naturally), and well, you know the carnage that can be sown and reaped.

Like your stubborn streak, my temper can work for or against me. Its line is well documented, and I grew up hearing tales of this temper being turned loose by my paternal grandfather and other folks in his family.

There have been cultural studies on the Southern white male that indicate the temper comes from centuries of being "herding" folks, those protectors of the flock—at any cost—making one quick to take offense as a threat.

Can such lineage really explain things like that? I'm leaning toward a yes. But can it also give you an excuse to act like an idiot? Well, that's possible, too. Especially in my case. But trust me, I will never be ashamed of who I am or where I come from; like most, I *try* to control the flaws and cultivate the attributes, if I can find them.

At five-foot-nine, maybe my temper is a Napoleon complex. Honestly, I never knew I was short until you came along and grew to tower over me. I think you were age ten when it first happened. Go ahead, laugh at Shorty. You've been laughing about that a long time.

Add to my easily rattled cage the quote that "I hate losing more than I love winning," and you have a tasty recipe for temper stew.

Also, I have this strong sense of justice, if such a thing really exists anymore. I have pondered if that might be why I became a reporter, so that I could find comfort in writing about wrongs in the world, and my reporting did dabble in that, now and then.

Doggedness, even with anger, to right what one considers a wrong is not always bad.

I've seen your frustration with my curse. "Dad, why don't you just let it go?" you've asked.

"Because I am right," I replied.

You always rolled your eyes, and you were probably right, too. Sometimes both sides are right.

Ah, everybody always looks for an excuse for their faults. I am not. I'm just telling you the Taylor temper is there, perhaps why, and it likely always will be.

Know, too, that I see passion as good. It can show how much we care. Just don't let it make you turn green and run amok.

My personal coaching style was praise in public, criticize in private, and fight to the death for my players in front of the whole universe, a bit overboard, but it was all or nothing. I am going over the hill on the roller-coaster, so why not throw my hands up and enjoy the ride? My philosophy would tend to get a coach kicked out of a lot of games.

I will say this—often when I was tossed, the team would win, often coming from behind. I could take that as an ego stroke, which is a dangerous, dangerous thing to do. As reported, I am very much a don't-brag-on-your-dog-until-after-the-hunt kind of guy.

Was the team rallying around their coach? Nah, really, y'all were probably just better off without me. So much for my ego.

But know this, I loved my players, and still do. Maybe I should have loved them enough to show them how to behave better.

Coaching, teaching, and farming are in your blood. Fruits from such labors are most often a long time coming. And it usually comes in the form of a hug, a memory, a smile, a laugh, or a thank you. Art Buchwald said, "The best things in life aren't things." It's on the wall in my classroom. Buchwald's *things* are abstract in a way you can't put on a wall like a plaque, or in a bank like money. But you can carry them in your heart for a long, long time.

Temper or not, the best thing to do is the hardest thing—be kind. Even when you not only suffer fools, but when you are tempted to be the fool. The Greatest Teacher said, "Love one another . . ."

But some of us are cursed to going overboard in our caring, and sometimes we jump in a raging sea with no thought, much less a life preserver. And there, danger lies not in becoming wet, but in becoming the rage, the storm itself.

Are there positives linked to that temper? Maybe.

Loyalty? I'll fight to look after my family and friends.

Now is all that an excuse for bad behavior? No.

My advice. Continue to do better, and always try to act like your mom and other friends and relatives who have the secret to always acting kindly, or at the least behaving.

We all wear the label of sinner more than saint. By nature, we're prone to errors in everything, including in the titles we put on each other.

I believe our Maker has a scorecard, and all my errors are on it. The best I can anticipate is maybe, like I once heard singer and songwriter Ray Wylie Hubbard claim, "I can only hope He grades on a curve ... C plus ... maybe even, for some of us, a C minus."

You know I am not a saint. You've seen me in action. Fathers are often a son's first hero, until they realize Dad's flaws. We dads (parents) never really get the full cape back once children become teens, but children understand as they age. They tend to look even closer at parents and realize there were indeed times when they deserved the capes, and perhaps they were right to get mad and turn green now and then.

Honestly, there are so many chinks in my batting helmet, most from leaning into bad pitches and needless battles.

Age is advantage, sometimes. It can work wonders on a temper, and places one no longer needs to take it.

A bartender at a class reunion told me that. "Oh, I've seen many class reunions," the elderly bartender told me.

"Oh yeah, what did you and your classmates learn after much time had passed?" I asked.

"Humility. We all became humbler," she replied, offering a lot of wisdom in a small dose.

I didn't write it on a napkin, and it didn't famously go on to become an equally famous country song as is the cliché, but I did put it in my mental notebook.

Of course, old age forces our hand on such. Maybe we become better at sitting this one out, because that's all we can do.

But every now and then, it's also good to know I can still rage against the dying of the light, Mr. Blake, and anything else.

Please know I tell you all this so hopefully when you sit in your own yard chair along the sidelines, you might recall me as someone willing to take a tempered (and *Taylored*) stand for those he loved and what he believed.

"Out of the night that covers me,
Black as the Pit from pole to pole,
I thank whatever gods may be
For my unconquerable soul.
In the fell clutch of circumstance
I have not winced nor cried aloud.
Under the bludgeonings of chance
My head is bloody, but unbowed.
Beyond this place of wrath and tears
Looms but the Horror of the shade,
And yet the menace of the years
Finds, and shall find, me unafraid.
It matters not how strait the gate,
How charged with punishments the scroll,
I am the master of my fate:
I am the captain of my soul."

William Ernest Henley, "Invictus"

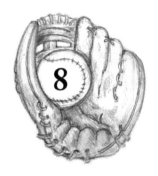

Invictus Means Unconquered

Dear Landon,

Post-accident, as I lay there in the hospital's darkest hours, sharing a small couch with your mom, and listening to the electronics to which they had you wired, I often silently recited the poem "Invictus" by William Ernest Henley.

Invictus means unconquered. By the way, that's also the title of a David Allen Coe cassette I listened to in high school. You may remember Coe from the song "You Never Even Called Me by My Name." That's the song that talks about the ingredients of a good country song: trains, trucks, prisons, and getting drunk.

You want a baseball connection? OK, a famed line from Coe says, "A friend named Steve Goodman wrote that song." Goodman did write it and even received uncredited help from John Prine. Both performers cut their teeth in Chicago, so no surprise Goodman was a Cubs fan (bless him). Goodman lost his life to leukemia, and some of his ashes were unofficially scattered at Wrigley. In addition to "The City of New Orleans," he wrote "Go Cubs Go" and "A Dying Cubs Fan's Last Request," which is worth checking out if you have the time.

But I wandered off the base path. Back to "Invictus": I have taught the poem for years to all my English classes.

I even have it on the wall behind my desk at school on a canvas picture of you pitching in the West Tennessee All-Star Game. You have a determined gaze and the black carbon prosthetic, used to help you grip a glove, is accented in the corner of the shot.

On the photo, I took liberty with Henley's words, however. Now, altering an author's or source's words is not something I was taught to do—ever—as an English teacher or a journalist, but I did it this one time because I kind of felt obligated.

I took "I thank *whatever gods may be* for my unconquerable soul" and changed it to "I thank *my God who loves me* for my unconquerable soul."

My reasoning is simple enough. After He helped us ford some deep water in the stream of Life, I figured we owed the Commissioner of the Game the recognition.

But again, there amid the great unknowing, the dark hospital room, the late and early hours, with your mom and I pondering and praying for your recovery, I began a ritual of saying "Invictus" in my head.

Mantra, chant, prayer? I am not sure, but it felt true and gave me comfort as the right words so often do.

This is nothing new for "Invictus."

Henley's poem has been famously used to inspire Nelson Mandela, Dr. Martin Luther King, and Sir Winston Churchill. Legend has it American prisoners of war in Vietnam shared it on toilet paper after using rat droppings as a pencil. I am not sure about that, but I feel oh so fortunate not to know about rat droppings or the toilet paper of Vietnam POWs. (Thanks, veterans!)

The story behind the poem, I learned as it haunted me in my hospital hymns, is that Henley wrote in near defiance. Like you, he became an amputee as a teen or nearly so. His leg had to be amputated from complications with tuberculosis. The poem is said to have been an inspiration and retaliation, in that the youngster would not give up or allow them to take his other leg. Reports are that a doctor named Joseph Lister, experimenting with germ-killing solutions, helped the cause of not losing both. Have you ever heard of Listerine? It is a mouthwash that still kills germs today.

It is also written that Henley was friends with Robert Louis Stevenson, who wrote *Treasure Island*. Stevenson is said to have based his most famous character on Henley. Long John Silver was a tall, pegged-leg pirate who didn't let his amputation interfere with his battles.

I also have long brandished a Stevenson quote on the wall of my classroom and sent it to close friends: "We are all travelers in the wilderness of this world, and the best that we can hope for in our travels is an honest friend."

In class, I point out the most important word is *honest*. "Good friends will not only tell you what you want to hear, but also what you need to hear," I pontificate, to rolling eyes, with mobile phones hidden in their laps.

Henley was also a friend of playwright J. M. Barrie. Henley's young daughter often referred to Barrie as her "fwendy," which led to the child becoming the inspiration for the character Wendy Darling in Barrie's play, *Peter Pan*. She was an only child and died at a young age.

As you may have learned, Life's stories are twined 'round influences by our acquaintances. I often pondered if it is a web or a chain.

But again to "Invictus." I think many readers claim the "I am the master of my fate; I am the captain of my soul" lines as their favorites. And I often say when teaching it, "Your soul is indeed something special. You really are the captain of your soul if you believe in free will. In my faith, God allows that. But decisions and the charted course of your soul are up to you. *God doesn't even control what happens to your soul.*" Some students look up from hidden cell phones when I say that.

But what are my favorite lines of this poem? As indicated by the print behind my desk, I tend to lean toward the "thank what gods may be for my unconquerable soul," even though I changed it. It shows an appreciation for an inner strength that a select few possess. A strength that, for me, can only be explained as divine.

Your life was spared via God's will, prayer, surgeons and germ-killing substances, scalpels, titanium rods, plates, and screws. You need a card to get through the metal detectors at the airport.

As I have watched you reach seemingly unconquerable goals and achievements through the storm of your life, one word comes to mind: *Invictus.*

The soul—your soul—is just that. You control it. Accidents, age, life in general can scar our body, but never does anyone else steer your soul, no one but you. You chart your soul's course, even where it ends up.

In the words of Disney's Captain Jack Sparrow—and a good game plan to continue—"Set sail and bring me that horizon."

Photo courtesy of Taylor Wilson
Beth and Taylor Wilson laugh with Landon after a win for his club team on the field at Arkansas State University.

"But there's a story behind everything. How a picture got on a wall. How a scar got on your face. Sometimes the stories are simple, and sometimes they are hard and heartbreaking. But behind all your stories is always your mother's story, because hers is where yours begin.

". . . I realized when you look at your mother, you are looking at the purest love you will ever know."

Mitch Albom, *For One More Day*

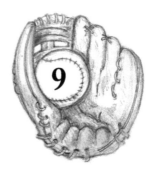

These Are the Hands

Dear Landon,

"Oh, he gets it all from his mother. Thank the Lord, he seems to have more of his mom's DNA than mine. I am the weakest link in this chain. Beth Wilson is the rock. Prayer works, and God is good."

These words, or something similar, are how I venture into a conversation about the success, astonishment, and wonder of your voyage through tribulations and recovery.

I tend to shed the light on the ones who I believe deserve it. I have always been guarded about enjoying success too much, even the smallest personal victory.

I may even take it to the extreme, so worried in the reality that something bad is bound to happen, that I sometimes neglect to enjoy the slightest moment in the sun for fear of clouds. So yeah, I am a self-professed Eeyore, whose famous weather report was, "We haven't had an earthquake lately."

But proof-positive that opposites attract, I married someone with the personality of a Tigger, and as Disney's version of that famed A. A. Milne classic claims, "The wonderful thing about Tiggers is that Tiggers are wonderful things."

Oh, God had us in the Storm, but your mother also helped show amazing grace.

She and many of the others on that side of your family hail from a region of our county known as Shepp Bottom, which was once called Shepherd's Switch for the train track.

I remember going on double dates and the folks riding with me to pick her up would say, about the time the pavement ended, "How did you ever find this girl?"

"Oh, I got lost looking for a coon dog down here once. Walked toward the light and Beth adopted me and the dog," I used to joke.

But the family legend is true—we met in second grade.

She claims I broke her heart when I walked up to her and gave her a paper one. It was in Mrs. Sybil Williams's second-grade class at East Side Elementary.

The story goes that she had a crush on me.

I know. I can't explain that, either. Who could? It was obviously an uncharacteristic lapse in judgment in her early years.

It was Valentine's Day, and I was handing out those heart-laced cards to classmates. And when I got to the little redheaded girl—I am SO like Charlie Brown—I said, according to her, "Here's your card! MY MOMMA MADE ME GIVE YOU ONE!"

Beth claims she was CRUSHED!

If I could take back one sin, of the many I have committed and will commit, that would probably be it. Still, it turned out all right for me, anyway. If I hadn't been such a mean little boy, we might not have ended up together, and your story would never be.

For better or worse, God gave us each other. When telling that story, I often point out the many morals, if not cautions, within. So, class, this is what we learned:

1.) Listen to your mother's intuition. Moms really do know best. My own mother knew I needed to give a card to the little redheaded girl. One simple act of kindness and look what I won, the big door prize. Beth may have changed her mind on her winnings.

2.) Never underestimate the desire of a woman to get what she wants. "Oh, I'll get him!" I can imagine the redheaded girl plotting. And she got me, all right, but along that same vein flows this ensuing lesson:

3.) Be careful what you wish for; you might get it—for better or worse, and sometimes maybe even much worse.

Sure, I gained the better end of the deal. A licensed counselor by trade, she either took me on as a field study of the senseless, or maybe it's another case of God taking care of fools. Maybe it was both.

* * *

Of all the memories of your mom through your Storm, one stands out more than the others.

A lot of people don't know, but you nearly lost your leg. You wear a shark-like scar today as proof. And deep down, I hope you tell your children how you fended off a great white while surfing the Baja Peninsula. No matter how you tell it, though, no story will be as worthy as the truth. Especially the part about your mom.

An amazing plastic surgery team used a unique procedure to get your leg to come together, as The Beatles would say. A surgical device, designed like the straps of a Roman sandal, encircled your leg. It could be wrenched tighter over time to help the skin grow back together.

Doctors also called for increased protein, to basically help the gaping leg wound heal. Protein helps repair muscle, skin, and other tissue. It also helps fight infection, balance body fluid, and carry oxygen through the body.

Allen Watts, our dear friend and a Sunday School teacher to us both (God bless him), saw this as a mission. How many times did he weave through rush-hour Memphis traffic to deliver you Central BBQ ribs and other items you had hand-picked throughout the city? We should call that limb the one that Allen (re)built.

Even today, Central BBQ smells like hope and friendship to me, and Watts and his family were a blessing to us in a bleak time.

Still, the possibility of you losing another limb was a lot to bear. It was a weight of unknown darkness, and it roamed the corners of my heart, mind, and hospital room for a while. If I mused about it too much, I could see the shadows of doubt growing crowded in the corners of the room.

And even later, you would say aloud and defiantly of the troublesome leg, "Just cut it off. I want to go home."

You would have never made it back to the pitcher's mound had this procedure not proven a well-plotted course.

Your mother, the one who made that mistake and married me, would stand no nonsense. It was at that time in the ordeal that Beth would stand and deliver.

In reflection, the brief but powerful event may have been one of the turning points of so many things to follow.

I do know the vibe was never again the same. Beth's tougher than the famed pine knot, and it ain't bragging when I tell folks, you share her genetics. It's an honor on your pedigree papers. I believe her remarkable resolve saved your leg and maybe my sanity.

So listen closely:

I swear, I saw her take a surgeon's hands into hers and dole out the will of God.

It doesn't take much to recall the memory. It's as fixed in me as my love for you both.

There we were discussing your leg and the gaping wound it wore.

Dr. Roberto Lachica, the team leader, was surrounded by his staff. And like so many surgeons, there was an aura about them. I like to imagine it is not unlike the air of preflight fighter pilots. There was just this unsung sentiment, "We're going to battle, and we're fighting, regardless. It's business. It's what we do. We can tell you the target, but we can't tell you any certain results."

Still, before they would all fly off into the unknown, Beth told the talented squadron leader Dr. Lachica to give her his hands, and then she told them all, "I don't know if you believe in God or not. But these are the hands that God's going to use to save my son's leg."

It was a so-let-it-be-said, so-shall-it-be-done moment if there ever was one. If nothing else, it was as bold a claim as I had ever witnessed. Landon, I tell you that only a mother could do this, and just maybe, only *your* mother.

When she said it, a hint of humanity showed in the lead surgeon's steely, fighter-pilot eyes, and I imagine it's not something they can afford to show trauma-center families in preflight mode. Maybe it's for insurance reasons, just as no one is ever deemed cured of cancer; they're instead said to be cancer-free.

Or maybe surgeons must be methodically machine-like to protect their own hearts, in the event of the occasional and inevitable crash/failure.

Many things can't be claimed certain.

But Beth Wilson, the Shepp Bottom native, and the redheaded girl I knew since second grade, spoke as if she knew.

My memory of this proclamation is a memory as forged and founded as the Rock of Gibraltar. (Here's where you need to go back and see number 2 in my morals list, above.)

When she unleashed that dose of daring faith, I didn't look at the others. I didn't scan the corners of the room for the shadows, either. The shadows had to have packed up and left.

Honestly, I didn't look at anyone else, because I was afraid that they'd all see my doubt. But even if any of it had bled out of me, such haunted doubt and darkness no longer had a chance. Her faith had unbridled a Light that rid the room of it all.

I really stood amazed at my wife's mic-drop performance. Who could follow that? So I (ever the dad/Charlie Brown dumbstruck with awe for the redheaded girl), mumbled something and offered the surgical squadron some of the excess candy people had brought you. Perhaps they could take it home to their children. It was around Halloween, and they did.

And that's a sweet ending for this letter, because we now know God was looking after me when He allowed your sweet mother to be duped into taking me on as a lifelong project. And if He is looking after me, He's looking after you.

You need to know, *you should be forever grateful to her. I am.*

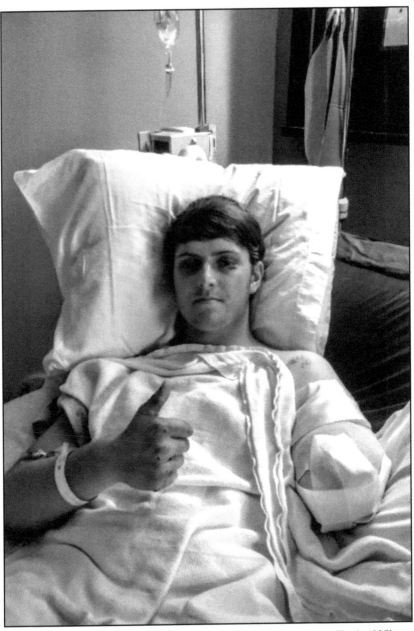

Photo by Taylor Wilson

Only a day or two after the accident, Landon already planned to return to the field.

"... The smell of hospitals in winter
And the feeling that it's all a lot of oysters, but no pearls
All at once you look across a crowded room
To see the way that light attaches to a girl ...
"And it's been a long December and there's reason to believe
Maybe this year will be better than the last
I can't remember all the times I tried to tell myself
To hold on to these moments as they pass ..."

Counting Crows, "Long December"

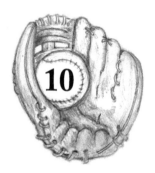

Hospitals and Humanity

Dear Landon,

The longer we stayed in the hospital, the more aware I became of things around me. The cloak of what happened was still burdensome; as a parent, I know some of that weight will never go away. But in the weeks that followed the accident, I began to be able to carry the weight easier. Maybe mentally, the shock simply waned, and scars were forming some padding.

God, prayers, family, and friends helped.

Your care, comfort, and healing remained center stage, but it was easier to begin noticing my surroundings.

Light, or maybe it was hope, began to grow faintly in a place first only seen as gloom, doom, and the "horror of the shade," as Henley had written in his poem, "Invictus."

Your stay became much more of a waiting game, waiting on your leg to heal, primarily.

There was even a hometown connection within the walls. Bobby Barden, from our hometown and a fellow Mississippi State dad, worked in the ER as a surgery technician. His kindness and shared information about your condition and surgeries were priceless. Another comforting family friend, Stone Taylor of Ripley, Tennessee, was a nurse intern at Regional Medical Center during that time.

The connections continued. Years later, the benefits of these small-town links connected us, would be passed along, and prove helpful after another horrific accident when your friend Sam Banks was in a terrible auto crash. Sam got a chopper ride, too. We are blessed Sam is still with us.

Meanwhile, if visitor traffic slowed, I began to wander about, to and from the car, the cafeteria, and Starbucks. How easy is it to become addicted to Starbucks? Your mom and I found out.

As the fog lifted some, surroundings became more noticeable. I fell into my nature as an old journalist/storyteller. My routine trips out of the room were mostly to the destinations mentioned, or maybe to escort someone to their car or the elevator, but I also often went to the chapel to pray.

In these walks, I began to people-watch, noticing faces and reading them somewhat. If you looked closely enough, you might detect those with loved ones in-house and at what stage of their stay they were going through.

Shocked. Sad. Dazed. Hopeful. Accepting. Content.

Largely, people were broken down into employees, visitors, and those caring for their loved ones. The eyes are the window to their souls, should one care to look.

Sounds, smells, vibes. All the things that define a place were all about. I had a tough time admitting it, but gradually I began to see it all tied into some sort of knot that I could call nothing more or less than beauty.

Say what?

Yeah, I wrestled with that conclusion, too.

This was the interpretation of a clearing mind (mine): A trauma center, and perhaps any hospital to a degree, is basically a battle for survival—between life and death, with the ill loved one caught betwixt and between.

Now, this beauty is much harder to see on Ground Zero, where the battle is very much blood, guts, and adrenaline, but it's there, too. The urgency for the task at hand blurs it, but this radiance may even exist here in its most pure form.

Humans fighting the good fight to help humans.

But again, with all the loss. The death. The blood. The gore. The possibilities for life-changing/altering/stopping horror. How can this be beautiful?

It's collateral beauty. It's the good that's hard to see because of the damage being done. Trust me, it's there, nonetheless. You may have to look through a lot of tears to see it. You may need time for scars to heal and cushion your heart. But if you look, you can see it.

This principle was reaffirmed for me by a movie of the same name starring Will Smith. Maybe it was a Godwink, but after we got home, I happened upon it, and I basically saw the same line of thought that had invaded my mind back at the hospital.

In the movie, *Collateral Beauty*, a character representing Death points out—in a hospital—that one must see the beauty in all things, even the seemingly horrific like death.

Was this art imitating (my) life or vice versa? I don't know. I had never seen the movie. Maybe God thought I needed to hear that message again to reiterate and allow it to soak into my simple mind.

By the way, the critics panned the movie, which, of course,

means I think it's good. Maybe I should go back and see it again.

Astronomer Carl Sagan wrote of a blue dot . . . a pinhead of blue in a vast ocean of black. He points out, way more eloquently than I, that this dot is Earth/us out there floating in an immeasurable wasteland of a sea. Everything that is human—good, bad, indifferent—can only happen on that blue dot.

The dot is all we got, really. So be kind, show compassion for one another.

There's a beauty in it.

Hospitals heed this call. Amid the horror and potential for tragedy, there are specks of humanity, with endless possibilities for kindness.

Dear Landon,

I just wanted to write you a note of best wishes and good luck. I understand that you had a pretty bad accident recently and I know that can be incredibly tough, but my experiences have taught me that with courage and strength you will be able to move beyond anything that might stand in your way.

You may not know much about me but I faced similar circumstances when I was your age. I was born missing my right hand. I never wanted to make a big deal about that, and I still don't, because I don't think it really was that much of a problem. I just had to learn to do things a little bit differently than other kids my age. Even tying my shoes! It just took a little creativity, and belief and I was on my way.

That is not to say that things will always be easy. Certainly when you do things differently, there will always be extra attention. Sometimes there will be awkward questions and second glances from people who don't understand. In spite of that, I believe you will find that you have the courage and strength to make it through those moments. Tough challenges make tough people and you have to believe you will always be up to this challenge. When you gain this knowledge and this strength, you will find that those tough times seem to pass by more quickly, and bother you a little bit less as time goes by.

This all may be a bit too much coming from someone you don't know but maybe it helps to know that I once played in the Major Leagues! You see even though I grew up with one hand, I always believed that I could play games as well as my friends. As time went by that turned out to be true and I ended up playing baseball all the way until I made it to the big leagues... I played at the University of Michigan, and for the Angels, White Sox, Yankees and Brewers

If I can do it... Landon you can do it! With creativity, belief and determination you will find there isn't anything in this world you can't do. Just keep believing that... keep believing you are up to any challenge!

I hope when things start to get better you will have a great Holiday Season! Stay tough whenever you feel down. Nothing can stop you!

I will be rooting for you.

Your Fan,

Jim Abbott

Merry Christmas Landon

May 2018 bring you great joy

*"The days I let my gratitude
exceed my expectations are very good days."*
Ray Wylie Hubbard, "Mother Blues"

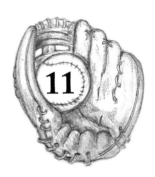

Inspiration and Gratitude

Dear Landon,

A
s a teacher, I have found that offering up the right words
of inspiration at the right time has the potential to work
wonders.

You and I have been fishing on windless days, right? You know,
those days when the water looks like slate.

Well, inspiration can be like tossing a bass plug out there into
all that smoothness. It creates ripples that travel outward in circles,
hopefully touching and changing lives as it moves.

As noted, people showed up. Friends and family by the hundreds
inspired you to heal, fight, and not give up. But others came loaded
down with encouragement from unexpected places and people
whom we didn't even know.

For some reason, people who heard your story felt moved to
reach out and help.

And each contact was a blessing.

Several people with like injuries or lengthy hospital stays took their time and traveled a long way just to visit, look you in the eye, and say, "Hey, you can do this! I survived something similar, and you can, too."

Again and again, this happened—an outpouring of compassionate folks, too many to name or recall without fear of leaving someone out.

One example of this inspiring phenomenon is when Tim Corbin, head baseball coach at Vanderbilt University, gave you a call. He would later likewise be kind enough to get you tickets to see Vandy play the school you now attend, Mississippi State University.

Jonathan Estes from Freed-Hardeman University also made a trip to see you.

Former Union University baseball coach Andy Rushing would also come to visit you and later follow up with a visit to our home.

I knew Coach Rushing, a wonderful leader, from when I attended Lambuth University way back when. He encouraged you to achieve your goals and stay involved in sports whether playing or coaching. Coach Rushing, also a great storyteller, mentioned a Union golfer who had returned to play after being severely injured in the tornado that once tore apart the campus. Like you, this injured athlete was also found at the scene by his uncle, who I believe Coach said was a paramedic or firefighter.

Fellow teacher Robert Mathis even got word of your story to former MLB pitcher Jim Abbott, who famously played his career without a hand.

Abbott took the time to send you a lengthy letter with several signed baseball cards and a photo.

"If I can do it . . . Landon, you can do it! With creativity, belief, and determination you will find there isn't anything in this world you can't do. Just keep believing that . . . keep believing you are up to any challenge!" Abbott said in his letter.

We have it framed in our home, along the stairs to your room.

I have wondered if Abbott ever knew the rest of your story. Like all these folks and so many I haven't mentioned, Team Wilson hopes they all know their inspirational efforts helped you achieve your goals.

"There are no random acts ... We are all connected ...
You can no more separate one life from another
than you can separate a breeze from the wind."

The Blueman, Mitch Albom's novel,
The Five People You Meet in Heaven

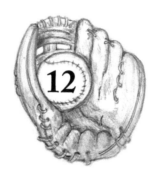

Connections

Dear Landon,

I've long thought connections are strange and wondrous things, and it was obvious in our experience with your accident.

Everyone has a story to tell. It is especially strange to see how the stories, and how we humans, are all entwined and influence one another. Maybe it's that old seven degrees of Kevin Bacon game. Maybe it's the internet.

But I do believe "It's a Small World" carries a lot of weight. It's the Sherman brothers' most played song ever, fifty million-plus times and counting, according to some sources.

Its lyrics, considering the COVID-19 pandemic, seem more heavy metal than Disney-like, though:

"It's a world of laughter
A world of tears

It's a world of hopes
And a world of fears
There is so much that we share
That it's time we're aware
It's a small world after all."

It says a lot about perspective.

Regardless, the world often does seem small and getting smaller when we make miraculous connections. It also seems to me to be planned. I say this a lot because I see it a lot. Yeah, yeah, redundancy or an insurance ad slogan (get it?). Hidden dad joke, right?

As the one-time agnostic Morrie Schwartz, of *Tuesdays with Morrie* fame, came to realize and say in his final days: The world seemed too perfect to be an accident.

Are any meetings, chance or otherwise, accidents in our small and getting smaller world?

As we tried to survive the trials of the accident, I often had moments that could be labeled anything from "ah-ha" to gobsmacked, or maybe I was God-smacked, which I like to think of as much stouter than a Godwink.

Let me give you a few examples.

There came a time during your hospital stay when hospital rules would not allow more than one person to stay in the room with you. I know these rules were being bent elsewhere, as nurses told me so. Detesting being late, I got there early one morning, and an administrator came in and chewed politely on me for breaking the rule. Since I didn't break the rule, I chewed back, not so politely. Sorry I upset you and your mom.

Anyway, I had to find somewhere else to stay. A hotel for that length of time was going to be costly, and I know very few folks who live in Memphis whom I would have bothered with such.

Out of the famed blue—and gray, go Tigers!—an old University of Memphis friend, Jody Callahan, contacted me after hearing about the accident.

We had not seen each other or talked in years, but there's this great thing about friendship; it stands the test of time. Even regardless of team affiliation. He's a Cubs fan.

When we were kids, Jody and I wrote for the *Daily Helmsman*, the UM college paper. We won an investigative reporting award of some sort. And in reflection, I am sure it was because of Jody's talent more than mine.

* * *

Also, side note: While working on the *Helmsman*, I remember writing a feature story on a wheelchair athlete group then called the Bluff City Rollers. It helped shape my thoughts on those with disabilities, and I remember one of the members laughing and saying something like, "If there's a way to pole vault in a wheelchair and members want to try it, we're all in!"

I also recall the influence of the late Spence Dupree, who was wheelchair-bound from an early age but never let it get in his way. He influenced me as an outdoor writer and as a pioneer for attacking the world regardless of difficulty.

Both those connections helped me gain perspective for folks with disabilities.

* * *

Though we have rarely seen each other since college, Jody is and always will be my friend. And as such, he contacted me asking about you. It also just so happened that a friend of his had parents with a rental house they weren't using. I was welcome to it.

It couldn't have come at a better time, and he met me there to show me the home.

"Oh yeah, these folks once lived in Brownsville, our hometown; they said they are glad to help and treat this home like it's yours," Jody said, giving me the keys.

Previously unbeknownst to anyone, not only did the homeowners once live in our hometown, but through business they also knew many of our relatives, including your grandfather.

I went inside, took a pistol out of my pocket, and put it near a Bible on the coffee table. I guess you could say I was covered.

There were crosses and a few other Christian-themed decorations around. It was a welcome home away from home for a God-smacked dad.

Your mom and I keep a cross the Combs family gave us on a shelf in our home today.

* * *

The first time I met Brandon Rowland, he was around ten or twelve and playing tennis on his knees. He had to because he'd lost his legs to a rare disease several years earlier. That he was playing on his knees was not as amazing as the fact that he was alive. The disease that claimed his legs kills nearly all who have it.

But Brandon is not one to listen to the odds, especially those that go against him.

Sound familiar?

Young Brandon would run through a pair of knee pads every other week or so. Eventually, he'd graduate to prosthetics and today works for a company that specializes in legs.

I worked with his mom, Mary Pat, at the *Jackson Sun* in Jackson, Tennessee. I talked her into letting me take Brandon hunting and fishing because it would be something he could "do as he got older and could no longer compete in sports," I remember saying.

He loved the outdoors, and it's an addiction he and his family still blame me for today.

I think I even prayed/called up his first deer. It was unusually cold. And he couldn't stay in the deer stand and tolerate the weather.

"Let's go sit in the truck parked in the field," I said. "Sometimes they step out of the thicket and look at the truck."

Brandon said OK through chattering teeth.

As we sat in the truck, I prayed: "God, I know you got that whole-world-in-your-hands thing going on, but could you help this kid get a deer?"

The prayer hadn't left my mind before a small buck walked down the fencerow right beside the truck. We rolled down the window, I talked Brandon out of buck-fever, and the rest is history.

Not sure of the legality of shooting a deer from a truck parked in a field, but maybe with God on our side, a ticket won't be forthcoming, either that or the statute of limitations may have us covered.

"If anybody asks, you shot that deer at 200 yards running," I remember laughing and telling Brandon. I have no idea how he tells the tale today.

I would also later see him shoot his first banded duck, which seemed to fall out of the sky just for him alone. I put the photo on the cover of a magazine I worked for at the time.

But as for my oh-so-shrewd prognostication of him giving up other sports and likely falling behind the pack, well, your dad was *wrong again*, (Bobby Boucher). But that's OK, I don't mind eating that kind of crow.

He went on to become a national wheelchair champion in basketball and an incredibly gifted golfer. I even attended the ceremony when he was named to the Jackson-Madison County Sports Hall of Fame. I think he's collected some other HOF titles since. He's somebody now, and even lowers himself to call me now and then! And yes, the night of his HOF induction, I admitted to his friends and family my prediction of him having to give up sports other than hunting and fishing. They laughed at me. I deserved it.

Within days of your accident, I called Brandon and told him about it and the loss of your limb.

Like my dear friend Jody, he showed up. How much of life is about that? Simply showing up and being there?

And I think God was there, too, with another heaping helping of smack for yours truly.

"Landon, when I was a little kid, they told me I would never walk," Brandon said not long after his arrival at the hospital. "Well, in case you didn't notice, I walked in, and if something weird doesn't happen between now and the time I leave, I am going to walk out. Watch me! You may not be able to do the things as you did them before, but you will be able to do them differently."

Now Brandon is a salesman, an excellent smooth talker, and a motivator with a gift for the gab. But sometimes, I still get misty-eyed when I recall that story and know well the seemingly random connection between Brandon and me.

Afterward, I called Brandon and asked if he thought it was an accident that we'd met that day on the tennis court. I don't remember what he said, but I know what I think.

Landon, people come in and out of our lives for a reason. Maybe, it's just for a second, but there's always a reason or, at the least, an opportunity for such meetings to end up miraculously meaningful. There's also always the chance for you to say or do something that may turn out surprisingly inspirational in the long haul. And, if you're lucky, there may come a day for you to do something extraordinary—help a friend in need.

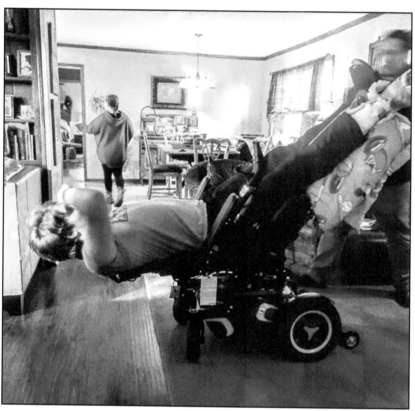

Photo by Taylor Wilson

Landon stands on his head in his electric wheelchair. Leaving it behind was an early goal.

*" 'Why did you do all this for me?' he asked. 'I don't deserve it.
I've never done anything for you.' 'You have been my friend,'
replied Charlotte. 'That in itself is a tremendous thing.' "*

E. B. White, *Charlotte's Web*

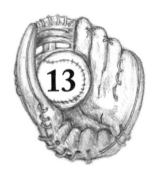

Foul Ball/Foul Weather Friends

Dear Landon,

"A lifelong friendship can start with a simple game of catch," is a Baseballism.

Heck, according to rock 'n' roll lore, the band Lynyrd Skynyrd met on a baseball field. How cool is that?

Word of your accident mobilized your army of friends, some from school, many from your teams and former teams. And you know what? Many showed up on the front lines.

I always saw you as nothing less than loyal. It may be the one and only positive trait that came from my gene pool. Everything else good comes from your mom. Then, too, in a near fifty-day hospital stay, we were much closer to the end than the beginning before your mother would even leave the hospital. So my good-trait contributions are still most likely nil.

But what a character trait loyalty is.

I remember you once demanding to go see a friend late one

night. This friend had an auto accident and was at Regional Medical Center in downtown Memphis.

"He knows nothing about the dangers of being around that Memphis medical center late at night," I remember saying to your mom. Little did we know, we'd all become much more educated.

As a pitcher, you weren't above payback for a wrong done to a teammate. You were one who would come out of the dugout to help if tempers flared.

Such reward for your loyalty and simple friendship was seen in the onslaught of your baseball family and so many others. Teammates, parents, and coaches from teams present and past showed up.

As travel-ball parents, your mom and I were often slyly criticized for being on the road playing ball all the time. And maybe, a time or two, even we pondered the many roads we covered.

But in the end, we were so glad to have been all in. "He loves it. He's young. This is what he does, and in turn it is what we do. If it were underwater basket-weaving, well, get us some strips of tree bark and snorkels," I often said.

True, we spent a fortune on baseball. But honestly, we would have spent it on whatever else you could have become equally interested in. How much would an underwater-basket-weaving pool have cost, I wonder?

But the friends you and our family made from all over the Mid-South cannot be weighed or measured. And never were these friendships of more value or more evident than when you were injured.

To try to name a list would be impossible and unfair. Some memories that do stick out, though, were visits from various coaches at all levels: college, high school, club, travel ball, and youth league.

One memory is of a photograph of former teammate Collin Fletcher scratching your back. It was an itch you couldn't quite reach with one arm. I sent the photo to Collin's dad Jeff with the caption "What friends are for," and Jeff replied, "He'll probably pick Landon's nose before he leaves," or something like that.

Overall, some hospital staff frowned upon the increased visitor traffic, and it would never even have been possible in the time of COVID. I can only shudder at the thought of what it would have been like had the timing of a bad situation been worse.

Your mom often politely reminded the hospital staff that you were a teen and prone to wanting to be in groups. She also asked them for some patience and understanding.

In reflection, I understand the frowns from a few staff members. There were people who were critical all around. Many were in worse condition than you and with an inevitable end in sight.

At one time, your room was sandwiched between a man who took a flu shot and went comatose for months and an epileptic who passed out and was fed upon by his pet pit bulls.

But you—only months into year eighteen, a social time for most—saw friends as critical to your healing. Your parents did, too.

Often, the party was in your room.

I guess too much joy can be a bad thing when sandwiched in such situations. Usually, the staff did a good job of tolerating the extra traffic and celebration of "I'm still alive!"

Of course, your friends from outside the foul lines arrived, too, and offered equal support. I cannot neglect them in telling this tale, even though the backdrop of this story is so predominantly baseball.

I hope you still count each friendship a blessing.

Video clips on social media made the rounds. There was one that got a lot of play of you shooting a NERF basketball repeatedly into a makeshift goal from your hospital bed. Another one was made of the first time you had gotten to go outside after weeks enclosed in four walls.

Fellow baseball fan and friend Clark Converse was with you

on that adventure. He filmed you taking the parking lot by storm, with the chant of "LET'S GO OUTSIDE!" And you quickly quipping the one-liner, "Oh no, please don't push me in the street! Not the street!" Again, you were poking fun at your predicament.

A sense of humor always helps heal. I hope you never lose it, even on your worst days.

It also helped the never-ending recovery party that at one time, you had a room to yourself, and it was routinely filled with teens.

"Wait a minute, that guitar is not electric is it, Adam?" I remember asking your friend, Adam Currie. "You know we don't need to get kicked out of here. We have nowhere else to go," I said.

Later in your stay, you and friends would roam the halls and outside sidewalks, with you in an electric wheelchair.

"Well, I saw Landon down on the sidewalk," said the director of the unit where we would spend our final weeks.

"He's really getting used to that electric wheelchair," I noted.

"Yeah, he had his electric wheelchair elevated so that it appeared he was standing on his head . . . and he was doing circles," the man said, ripe with implications that such actions needed to stop. Perhaps he didn't want the hospital held accountable for anything.

"Doughnuts. Those circles are called doughnuts," I said, unsure of the look on my face. I am sure it was shock at first, but I imagine admiration followed. I hope the director didn't catch the gleaming eyes and smirk of pride before he walked on by.

The staff repeatedly confirmed they had seen nothing like the outpouring of visitors, letters, and love.

And it wasn't just your friends and family who showed up. So did friends of your mom and mine.

Years later, we are still humbled and grateful for those who simply showed they cared, whether in person, or via a phone call, a card, etc.

Then high school vice principal and coach Tim Seymour brought down a huge banner of a get-well card that had hung in the school for people to sign. Many encouraging messages from school friends who could not get to Memphis were written upon it. We wrapped it around the wall of your room.

Your mom compiled a list of people who came to see you, and the list numbered well over 300 visitors. I am certain there were nearly as many more whose names were not recorded on the list.

The response via US Mail was similar.

The staff said they had never seen anything like it.

People constantly stressed the good attitude you had throughout the ordeal. A large part of this, I think, was through the incredible support you got from friends and family.

When you're eighteen, your friends are everything. And near the end of your stay, it was your friends you so wanted to return home to see.

But despite doctors' approvals, our discharge had gotten caught up in paperwork. It seems some branch of an insurance company farmed out some services to another insurance company that we could not reach for approval.

The hospital administrators said we couldn't leave until we got the nod from that company. It was getting dark, and we'd been packed and ready to go since morning's first light.

"I tell you what, they can either let me go home, or I am about to put this electric wheelchair on I-40. I want to go home and see my friends," you said in frustration.

Maybe they let us go because I played a wild card. Your mom and I were talking to administrators in the office, and they were stalling.

I was on the phone. Finally one of them asked, "Who are you talking to?"

"Our lawyer," I replied.

So they let us go home.

It's at this time that I'd like to thank another family friend, attorney Michael Banks.

Sleeping in our own beds never felt so good.

Even today, I'm still awed at the response, and I wonder why so many people showed they cared.

Were we a novelty?

Was it your attitude?

Was it that God knew we needed it?

I mean some people we didn't even know showed up. Some would even come from other parts of the hospital.

Often there would be a knock on the door and, "Hello, you must be Landon. I heard about you and wanted to come see you. I work on another floor . . ." was the way several conversations started.

It all was inspiring. And I also believe the outpouring fueled your success. We were blessed more than we realized in what could have been a very dark time had so many friends not showed up with large doses of comfort and love.

These friends helped you heal both mentally and physically.

Our family will be forever in their debt.

"How many slams in an old screen door?
Depends how loud you shut it.
How many slices in a bread?
Depends how thin you cut it.
How much good inside a day?
Depends how good you live 'em.
How much love inside a friend?
Depends how much you give 'em."
Shel Silverstein

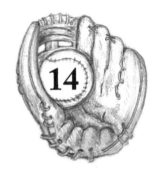

The Scary Part

Dear Landon,

The county road we live on is dangerous and has a reputation as such. No shoulders, ditches on the sides, hills, several sharp curves.

So I guess there is no surprise the road has seen its share of tragedy. We are not far from town, but when people drive it, they begin to feel like they can speed up—since they are now out in the country. I guess the same could be said of all country roads, though.

Having bought the family home and lived here most of my life, I am aware of several accidents. When I was a kid, I heard a wreck, walked down the drive, and looked to see an overturned vehicle and a body in the road.

I went and got my daddy, and we went up to the scene. A lady had died. My father covered her with a towel. The driver, disoriented after the wreck, had already gone miles in the other direction for help when we arrived. There were no mobile phones.

I also heard another wreck that killed a teen on the other side of the hill from where you were struck. It was a one-car accident.

And, of course, you and your uncle both were injured on the hill. Though your uncle's accident was not on the road, it was awfully close to yours.

Road sites get nicknames for accidents. Deadman's Curve, etc.

Now, imaginative, I have thought much of this. Maybe it's in my constant search for an explanation. The tragic events that I know of in my lifetime began north and seem to have worked their way south, toward town.

Why are some places seemingly tragic? Is some sort of residual impression left on such places, like dangerous roads, hospitals, battlefields, prisons? Such are the places paranormal teams visit. But also note, they most often call them ghost hunters, not ghost finders.

Is it a magic, a mojo, some mystical force?

Probably not, but if you have the storyteller's imaginative mind (a blessing and a curse) and you want a ghost story, I just gave you the beginning of one.

* * *

Ah, and what's one more story for a storyteller? I mentioned the hospital as a typical site for would-be haunts.

Now in our stay of months, I often roamed the halls on errands. And there were places that just felt different when you walked through them, especially when one was solo and not distracted.

Cool, goose pimples, hair rising, etc. Now, it wasn't riding-the-Big-Wheel-down-the-hall-of-the-Stanley-Hotel-in-*The Shining*, turn-the-corner-and-there's-the-twins creepy, but it was something there.

Once, traversing betwixt and between the hospital's network of halls and buildings, I came upon this couple. And immediately I knew they were celebrating something. Both were elderly; one wore the attire of a veteran. They were absolutely delighted to see each other, as if they had not seen each other in years. I don't know how I knew this, but it was something I just understood instantly, and from a distance.

But get this, they were doing the tango. Yep, I swear, right there in the narrow hall they danced. And you know me, so as a person a bit touched in the topknot, I also heard in my head the familiar tango music. In my memory, I swear, was "Por Una Cabeza" from a movie, *Scent of a Woman*.

The light was coming in from a lofty, lone, raised window, and it cast sort of a peculiar spotlight on their dance.

They totally ignored me, until I stepped into their light.

"Can I take your picture?" I said abruptly.

The question came from years of being a photographer. After a while, you kind of just see photos, not unlike that kid just saw dead people in *The Sixth Sense*. But when you see a photo, you also see it as a chance for a trophy of sorts. And like fishing, you always regret the ones that get away. I have many regrets of photos I didn't take in my crazy brain, too. So, even today, if I see what I think will make a good photo, I always take the photo rather than regret it later. If I am taking the picture of people (or say, ghosts), I always ask permission.

And with every mobile phone also doubling as a camera, there is no better time to collect memorable photos than today. One is always ready to take a photo.

So, phone in hand, I asked the famed "Can I take y'all's picture?"

Silently they looked at each other, sharing a secret smile.

Did that old man wink?

Lost in each other, they shook their heads, and I really don't remember a word. I instantly realized my intrusion in their joyous reunion, and I moved on.

Farther down the hall, I got the urge to look back but already knew what I would see. You can probably guess. The couple I should have seen had become . . . nothing.

Were they ghosts?

Oh, they probably weren't spirits, specters, or shades, but I'm certain there was a rest of the story, and they didn't want me to be a part of it.

How they vanished so suddenly certainly intrigues me.

And what if they were shades? There's certainly a lot of coming and going at a hospital, especially one like that.

Maybe one spirit had returned to another. And what ghost lovers in their right minds don't prefer to celebrate being reunited for eternity with a tango?

Hey, you know, I just gave you two possible ghost stories, right? And all in one letter. Now, that's a bargain!

And yes, like all the best ghost stories, they are true.

The late Dr. Tim Sumner watches as Landon Wilson strikes balls in the cage. Sumner was a beloved mentor and friend.

> *"A teacher affects eternity; he can never tell where his influence stops."*
> Henry Adams

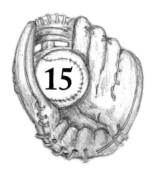

Coach, Teacher, Friend

Dear Landon,

The Game of Life is also filled with teachers (or the chance to be one). Some are wonderful characters who dole out blessings and challenges.

And for the ball player, well, you call your teacher coach.

One of your coaches, Dr. Tim Sumner, was a character and a blessing, and it was a challenge not to love and respect the man. He only stood along the foul lines of your life for a few seasons, but he made you a better player and, more importantly, a better person.

He started what would later become the family business, The Batters Box training facility, after initially teaching his children and others to hit in the family garage.

In addition to getting hitting instruction from Sumner, you also played for his club teams for three seasons. As with all your teams, along the way you made fast friends and memories.

The short, stout, fast-talking and -thinking Sumner grew up in the Midwest within blocks of the neighborhood that inspired Jean Shepherd to write *In God We Trust, All Others Pay Cash*, which in turn became the movie *A Christmas Story*.

Doc grew up not far from where Ralphie almost shot his eye out with a Red Ryder BB gun. Doc even had a few stories about the old neighborhood and kept some mementos from the movie on his desk. Because I was already a fan of the movie, Sumner's connection instantly gave the two of us a connection as well.

As a young man, he worked his way up the ranks as a successful high school teacher and coach. He got a doctoral degree in education at Mississippi State University. While earning it, he served as a grad assistant/coach with MSU teams that included Rafael Palmeiro and Will Clark (an era detailed in SEC Network's *SEC Storied: Thunder and Lightning*.) Doc even had his MSU Bulldogs coach's jersey in a frame at his office.

You would later choose to attend MSU. To this day, I believe Doc, along with my friend Mark Beason, showed you the way to Starkvegas: Cow Bell Central. One never knows when or how we have the chance to influence others.

Sumner also worked at the alma mater of Beth and me—the University of Memphis. His role there was student-athlete accountability. The way I understand it, his job was to help increase the graduation rate of student athletes and determine which recruits had a legitimate shot at graduating. Athletic graduation rates at UM were dismal at the time of his arrival. True to his nature, he helped turn the tide. But then, as I understood it, a one-and-done coach came along, who had just enough clout and wins to change all that, and Sumner was out of a job.

It was a one-door-closes, another-opens moment, and this paved the way for a bigger role in training youngsters at The Batters Box, which in turn would be how the Wilsons washed up in his batting cage that doubled as a Life Lessons classroom.

With Doc a die-hard Cubs fan and you bleeding Cardinal red since birth, the two of you enjoyed a relentless rivalry and took ruthless jabs at each other. The banter between you was entertaining in a World Wrestling Entertainment way. The rivalry was sheer show and entertainment. Those waiting for the next lesson often said they loved to listen to the two of you going at it.

Underneath, of course, you were bound tighter than the red seams of a baseball, and this time the hue was symbolic of something more than a team color. You shared a love and respect for the game and each other.

I really believe God gives us select individuals to help us around Life's base paths. I like to think Doc was handpicked by God—for your team.

And, oh yeah, your mother and I were paying Doc for the lessons, but I can't tell you the value of having a mentor like that to speak to you from time to time.

His lessons were sometimes bigger than baseball, which he respectfully called The Game.

For example, Doc even pointed out, believe it or not, there are things more important than The Game.

As a sophomore, you earned a lead role in the school musical, *The Sound of Music*, as Captain Georg von Trapp.

Now, I pre-pondered that the play would be held in spring, just when high school baseball was getting underway. I saw potential conflict. I knew if it came down to baseball or the play which would receive the nod from Landon Wilson.

And when spring arrived, there it was. An early-spring game was slated the weekend of the play. But Doc, a baseball guy if ever there was one, held you to task.

"When you took the part, you agreed to take on a commitment," Sumner told you. "This is your commitment; you need to stick with it. You don't sell your teammates out, be they on a stage, on a diamond, or in an office. I was even in a play once. The administration at the high school where I taught always wanted the coaches involved as well."

Well-rounded on nearly any topic, Sumner could discuss the storyline of *The Sound of Music* while also teaching you to hit line drives. A great teacher will use all hooks to hold attention.

Fortunately, it all worked out. Weather cancelled the game. Reviews raved, and as a dad, I admit you performed well.

As a pitcher, you felt natural at center stage. And your character was also married by a Cardinal. Well, at least the priest character that your teammate and buddy J. T. Lea was portraying wore Cardinal red!

I told someone once, "You know, Landon thinks I bring him to Dr. Sumner to teach him baseball. I bring him to Doc to make him a better person."

Doc's influence on your game cannot be denied. I sent you down there as a left-handed hitter who pulled everything to right field. It was all or nothing, down the right-field line.

He taught you religiously to hit up the middle and to opposite field. You became a thinking hitter. He also taught you that if it's not your pitch, don't swing.

"What if it's a strike?" I remember you asking.

"What if it's a strike you can do nothing with?" he replied. "You will still get out. The odds are better if you swing at pitches you know you can work with."

So his theory, day in and day out, was to swing at pitches you knew you wanted.

Hitting a baseball is the most difficult thing to do in sports, *USA Today* once reported. You get a hit three out of ten times in baseball and you are a Hall of Famer. You shoot 30 percent in the NBA or complete 30 percent of passes in the NFL, and you're out of a job.

Baseball is the famed "game of failure," and at the big-league level, a hitter does it repeatedly through a marathon of games, all for a lofty goal of 30 percent.

Sumner's efforts helped keep you most often at or near the top of the teams you played for in batting average, RBIs, and walks. You hit a lot of doubles, which may have been triples for someone not dragging size fifteen cleats around.

Sumner instilled untold patience at the plate. A parent at a high school game once said, "Landon sure does walk a lot." I replied that this was good and asked if he had ever read Michael Lewis's book, *Moneyball*. ("He gets on base.")

The same parent noted, "That has to hurt your batting average."

It doesn't; a walk doesn't even count as an at bat. Walking a lot was straight out of the Doc Sumner playbook: "If it isn't your pitch, DON'T swing."

Sumner relentlessly preached line drives, preferably up the middle or at the least to opposite field, depending on the pitch. Again, favorable odds: line drives get through. Flyballs and grounders are more often caught.

How many times did you hit a liner through the 5.5 hole (between third base and shortstop), made famous by Hall of Famer Tony Gwynn?

Like Doc, the famed hitter Gwynn was an ambassador for baseball. He also lost his life to cancer.

Gwynn is perhaps my favorite player outside of a Cardinals uniform. By all reports, he was a good person, as well as player. An *LA Times* sportswriter said of Gwynn's death: ". . . (T)he loss to the humanity of the sports world is incalculable . . . his greatest achievement was that he was so loved."

But despite Sumner's hitting instructions, you would finish solely as a pitcher in the end. It was the last place you would/could fit.

The mound would be where you made your last stand.

Specializing in one skill is also often a natural progression of play in The Game; players are staged to where they can perform the best.

Doc Sumner came to see you many times in the hospital. And once, in a still-haunting moment when I was walking him to the elevator, he said, "You know, what I teach Landon, I can no longer teach him," referring to the loss of your arm.

How I wish I had told him, "No, you're wrong! You're teaching more than hitting." But at the time I was so suddenly soul-crushed by that reality—that Sumner's lessons were gone—that my wits were beaten into silence.

Even today, when I pass through the route we used to take to Sumner's former business, that same twinge of regret hangs over me. Then I think of the good things he shared, and my heart beats again.

Still, with the realization that hitting was out, Sumner did not abandon you. He knew, as a pitcher, you still had a hook in the water. It just wasn't something he was best at teaching.

At a time where your doubting Thomas of a dad was gloom and doom, Doc showed up at the hospital with a newspaper article about another player who lost his arm and returned to the mound.

"It can happen," Sumner said in determined fashion. "And if it doesn't, well, Landon can still remain close to The Game and coach, if he chooses."

Good teachers always preach possibilities.

Doc was faithful with his hospital visits and generous with his time, always bringing doughnuts from his favorite bakery, and still doling life lessons, most marked with hope and joy.

He kept a photo of you portraying *The Sound of Music's* captain on his desk. I can't remember if you autographed it. That photo was right up there among all the other ball players, and that danged Cubs paraphernalia, of course.

I have a feeling he was equally proud of that photo as he would have been had you been in a Cubs uniform, or any of the other photos. Knowing Doc, he probably pointed to it in a lesson or two and talked about priorities. I know for a fact he used your story of perseverance as a lesson to other players.

Good teachers do that, too.

We first returned to his batting cage office when you were in an electric wheelchair.

Now, if it would have been me, which I say repeatedly, and I so literally wish it had been, I would not have been able to return, at least not so soon. To me, the memories seemed too raw. Maybe it was a dad thing. I would have dwelled on what was, but you always live for what is and what will be. (You're your mom's child.) True to your nature, you rolled into his office like you owned it and began trading Cardinals-Cubs jabs with your mentor and friend as if nothing ever happened.

My friend and fellow Batters Box parent, Nick Nicola, was there with his son Carson. He marveled at you, maneuvering that chair, healing and wheeling.

"I just don't know how he made it," Nick said.

I pondered how your mom and I did as well.

"God, prayer, family, and friends," I gave the familiar ingredients. "Well, that and the bumper of the vehicle that hit Landon wasn't made of Kryptonite . . . what with him being akin to Superman and all," I laughed.

Nicola and I had spent many innings together watching our kids play ball. I still consider him a good friend.

I know you returned a few more times to see Sumner at The Batters Box. You eventually even hit some balls in the cage with him. You told me you did OK, swinging with one arm.

I hate I missed the banter.

When we learned of Doc's illness, we all got in touch in various ways. I texted back and forth with family members mostly, not wanting to be a pest in such times.

Somewhere in my texts were these words, and a message I hope was relayed, "Tell him we love him."

The last I heard he'd made a turn for the better. My mind rested easy with, "Doc's going to be OK."

But Doc lost his battle to cancer.

Of course, we went to the funeral. I rode with my lifelong friend Jim Tyson, and you went with his eldest son, Drew.

Sumner was buried wearing a Cubs jacket and cap.

A lot of the players, family, and baseball folks he'd known and influenced were there waiting in line to pay respects.

Former Mississippi State University baseball coach Ron Polk, who literally wrote what's considered the book on coaching baseball, stood behind you in the visitation line.

You told me you talked to Doc Sumner not long before he passed away.

"If I'd known that was the last time, I would have said more," you added and went quiet.

I have a feeling I know what you would have told him—it would have been the things we should say so often to those we love and respect.

I know for a fact how badly you wanted to call him when Mississippi State University's baseball team won the College World Series in 2021. And, ah, what the heck, you'd probably take a shot at him about the Cubs, as any true Cardinals fan would do.

We can never repay Sumner for his part in your story. And in my scorebook, Doc's greatest achievement is like Gwynn's. In addition to being an ambassador for The Game, he left this world being *so loved*. We should all aim for as much before we touch Home.

Photo by Morgan Timms

Have arm, will travel. Landon boards the bus for an away game.

"And if only one thing had happened differently . . .
Sometimes we're on a collision course, and we just don't know it.
Whether it's by accident or by design,
there's not a thing we can do about it."

F. S. Fitzgerald, *The Curious Case of Benjamin Button*

No Keys to a Time Machine

Dear Landon,

Your accident happened on October 26. As a movie buff, you likely know that is the date igniting all the action in the original *Back to the Future*, when Doc first takes off in that DeLorean.

How many times have I pondered time travel since this happened?

How many times have I wanted to go back and change any of the events (even the smallest) that led to the accident?

Born with a wild and creative imagination, it's not hard for me to fathom the things I could do.

For example, one convoluted plan involves me going back in time and sitting in a deer stand to shoot out the driver's tires as he passes by. With my luck, I'd probably miss.

But I know you also considered this time-tweaking idea. I even heard you mention, while in your hospital bed, "It's like that scene in *Benjamin Button* where Daisy gets hit by the car." If there was only one thing you could have done differently on your run that night. You listed a few. Among them, you mentioned seeing our pastor friend Mike Young, and saying you thought about stopping to talk, but you didn't. Brother Mike would later visit with Brother Bob Connerley and pray with us in our home. Brother Mike would also later come watch you pitch.

There were several other things you noted that seemed small but would have been all it took to throw off the timing of events just enough. But as with the ballerina Daisy in *Button*, it didn't happen. She'd never dance again, but you would pitch.

You knew I was aware of that scene because I used it in class to point out cause and effect.

So, keeping it cinematic, movie buff, it still all makes me (and Forrest Gump) ponder the design theory. Is life a specifically grand design or destiny, like Lieutenant Dan thinks? Or are we all a feather floating on a breeze, or even as random as an unknown selection of chocolates, as Momma Gump thinks?

Forrest concludes it's both.

Me? I believe in a Designer, and if there is a Designer, there must be a design and vice versa.

Human, I so want it to be spelled out. And in the end, I must realize I will wrap my mind around it like I am a human, prone to great errors.

As my friend and teaching mentor Mary Jane Williams once pointed out to me, Isaiah 55:8-9 says: " 'For my thoughts are not your thoughts, neither are your ways my ways,' declares the Lord."

And again, human, I still must ask: Does God give us darkness to remind us of His light?

I don't know, but the Bible says He first created light out of the darkness. Can you have one without the other?

Of course, there is an age-old question: Why do bad things

happen to good people? How painful is it for me to say there is a reason for what happened to you? That's an answer you can't comprehend until you become a parent. But there has been some good to come out of the bad. We've seen it.

I have a video clip that the *Jackson Sun* shot of you. I sometimes send it to people, even today, saying not much more than, "Just in case you need to believe in the power of prayer, check this out." It is now years old and becoming somewhat dated, but I like to think it still makes a valid point.

In the clip you are on the field with your teammates, and you say you wouldn't change what happened to you because it has made you stronger.

So familiar with your body language, I am keen enough to see a distant glint in your eye when you say it, and I am proud beyond measure. But trust me, I *would* change it (even the will of God), and I have told you, flatly, I'd wished it were me so many times. I would trade places with you a thousand times. But we both know that isn't possible.

I have said I hope God explains to me why it happened one day if they let me in The Gate. I do have more good people up there "vouching" for me, that's for sure. And as time goes by, I sometimes see possible hints of understanding in my peripheral.

But by design, if you believe in such, God didn't choose me. He chose someone with the guts to handle it.

We're all on a collision course with something.

We can't change the collision, but we can control the mental state in which we survive it.

And that one thing—anything—that could have set things amiss so that the vehicle would not have struck you—well, it did not happen. All the dominoes fell horribly precisely for you to turn suffering into something that this baseball dad still thinks is amazing.

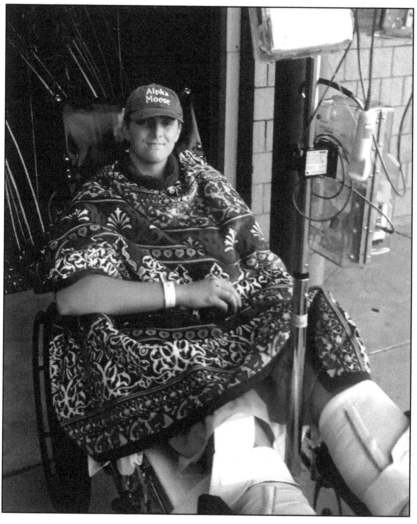

Landon goes outside for the first time in weeks during his stay at
Regional Medical Center in Memphis.

"Sometimes the only thing fair is a ball hit between first and third."

Unknown

Fair Ball?

Dear Landon,

It's an age-old question: *Why do bad things happen to good people?* You're human and prone to all our vices, faults, and negative things we do. No one is a saint. We are all sinners.

But overall, you're good, by my definition anyway, and you come from a good family, despite your dad, who has more faults than San Andreas and New Madrid combined.

But as you once said in defiance, and in the middle of some hospital predicament, probably waiting on a surgery: "You know I didn't do anything to deserve this, right?"

It was a good point when one looks around a trauma center, where obviously a lot of bad people are brought after they do bad things.

Now for me to tell you, as a parent, that it did not bother me that I had to sit and watch you suffer while people who had committed horrible crimes got medical attention would be a lie. Some were handcuffed to gurneys, for God's sake!

Often, if you know the background of a trauma center in a big city, you quickly understand that a lot of bad people end up there. The medical creed, though, includes caring for everyone who needs help. And that's what that amazing crew does there. I do not know how they steer clear of burnout or being overwhelmed.

Within the trauma center, there is a prison ward where all the criminals are kept while receiving medical attention.

Surgeries are logically done in the order of urgency, regardless of whether a patient is deemed good or bad by law.

One of your surgeries was put off multiple times. After you went without food or water for an extremely long time, I sought inside information, which you can get if you know people within the hospital. I discovered there had been thirty-something shootings in two days. All operations other than the most urgent were delayed. They simply did not have enough staff or workspace to keep up.

What was also reported to me was a gang war was going on within the city. If there was anything in the local media about it, I never saw it. But a lot of people were being treated for gunshot wounds in a short amount of time.

A twisted irony for the trauma center is that the health providers there become so good at what they do, partly because bad people are constantly harming others. As a result, the center's surgical teams get experience working on many severe injuries caused by the worst kinds of violence.

Meanwhile, my son waited in the wings for an operation that, as you said, you did not ask for or do anything bad to deserve.

Yeah, there's a parental anger in all that. That temper in me, the one that so often surfaces to reconcile what I see as unfair, it so wanted to surface. I really wanted to point out the seeming stupidity of it all. But who would listen, and what good would it do you? I could understand why bad things were happening to bad people.

But again, why do bad things happen to good people?

As a kid who asked a lot of questions, I once asked my mother that one, and specifically why God let it happen.

A teacher, she explained it to her child in this way: "God made things so they work, so they balance. Things are put in motion all as part of His plan. For things to work, for things to happen at best, His laws were put in place and these laws work as part of His plan. I believe it's for the best, whether we say it's good or not. For example, you can't jump off a building and expect to not fall, right? Gravity is a law, it can hurt you, but it also keeps you from flying off into space."

I also asked her once why people don't believe in God or are angry at him. At the time, I had begun to read a lot of Mark Twain, and most notably his seeming skepticism of religion, which was sarcastic at the least.

"You have to know that Mark Twain wrote that after the death of his child. Maybe he was angry and bitter.

"When bad things happen, we seek someone to be the cause, the reason. So why not blame the Ultimate Being? The obvious *human* thing is to blame The One in control . . . the one who put the laws into motion, right? It makes sense to us, but does it make sense to God? Maybe that is what we should think about."

Even with sage wisdom dumped on me at an early age and from an exceptional teacher, I still wonder about the logistics.

Maybe God tests those He knows can take it.

Maybe God takes the lives of some good people, seemingly early, because they're good enough to get where He wants them to be.

When we were nearing the end of our marathon stay at the hospital, a crew of doctors talked to us. And one took it upon himself to tell you something. It went kind of like this, minus quotations because it's from my memory:

Landon, I want you to know you are a good person, and you have a good family. I say this because, trust me, I work on a lot of what many will say are bad people—unbelievably bad (and these patients seem to work to prove it). That said, we are SO glad you have experienced such a remarkable recovery.

Typically, and I don't know why, but when the good people pass through our doors, they don't do as well. Is it twisted fate or irony? I don't know.

On the other hand, the hardest of cores, the meanest of mean, the so-called bad guys, will often thrive after treatment. I don't know why that happens, but it is often the case, and we see it a lot.

It even gets to the point sometimes where we are especially uneasy when good people arrive, because there is the unexplained phenomenon that they don't fare as well, even though we give everyone equal care.

All that said, we are all so happy you did well and are going home.

That was a proud moment for me, knowing you and your mom and the rest of the family, friends, and supporters waved an admirable banner, fought the good fight, and won. Really, I was simply glad to be somehow lumped in with all of you.

This is also where I piped in and pointed out my rural upbringing and my mutt-dog theory. Briefly, I told of a lifetime of good dogs and bad dogs and how often the worst seemed to happen to the best of dogs, while the mutts, mongrels, and strays plodded through the world unscathed, dodging farm equipment and all other life-threatening obstacles.

The medical crew turned and looked at me—the country bumpkin talking about dogs—nodded and smiled. I didn't look at you or your mom.

I imagine you knew; your dad often goes to the dogs.

* * *

As a side note on bad guys, as you know, you had eight surgeries. Many of them also involved going over your legs, making sure wounds were cleaned and rid of debris that might later cause infection. You had been through the process several times, and with each one, it was a lot like you were getting ready to pitch.

You would put on your headphones and get pumped up for the task at hand.

Once, out of the blue, you asked if one of us would go down and basically wait in the wings with you. Come to find out, the bad guys also waiting to go into their respective surgeries were confessing crimes to one another, and you were all in the same room.

And you, a smart kid, didn't want to have to be the only one to hear such criminal confessions, especially among criminals.

I am sorry you had to be put in that situation. That you had to be twice as fearful or concerned when going through what you went through.

After you told me about it, I thought to myself, "Surely they wouldn't remember you, anyway."

Fast-forward a few months, and we had a follow-up appointment. Your mom and I walked in behind you in your electric wheelchair. Two gentlemen were sitting outside discussing the ballistics of handguns, and what it had done to create their wounds. (I swear this is true.) And they looked at me, pointed at you, and said, "Is that the kid who was hit by the car?"

The hair stood up on the back of my neck, as I nodded and continued inside the office for our appointment.

Some patients could remember others.

Know this, the world has always had its share of bad people. And unfortunately, they have been finding ways to kill others or each other since Cain and Abel. But also know, there are sincerely good people in the world, and you had a world of them on your side.

Photo by Morgan Timms
Landon went through physical therapy sessions two to three times a week. The hardest work was getting his right foot to move up or down.

"One of these days, I am going to climb that mountain."
Randy Owens, the band Alabama; "Mountain Music"
Walter Brennan, "Old Rivers"

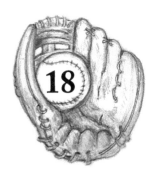

The Hero Picks a Path

Dear Landon,

We knew before we got home that we were going to need a van with a wheelchair lift to transport you around.

Of course, you would soon figure out how to wheel your electric wheelchair over to your own vehicle and transfer from chair to truck. Off you'd go in the seeming speed of light, a cloud of dust, and a hearty "Hi Yo, Silver!" Well, the Lone Ranger chant might be a stretch, but you did get back behind the wheel very soon. And my concern over what you would do if you needed to get out of the vehicle is useless now.

But for a while we needed a van with a wheelchair lift. Your grandfather had one, but he needed to have it to get back and forth to his own doctors' appointments, as he was fighting cancer.

The price of renting one versus buying and reselling was no comparison. We had to buy.

So I was in the market, and two of my old buddies, Ronnie

Belew and Chester Dixon, went with me to make the purchase. They didn't say it, but I know they went to make sure I got the best deal. Both have sound car knowledge. To me, it was a show of colors from these two gentlemen, though I know through countless hunting and fishing trips that they were always on my team. I wrote about some of our exploits in many columns over the years.

I can't repay them (and so many others) for simply being my friends. Do we ever have enough people who really have our back?

The van? It was nothing fancy. White. It looked like it could be an ice cream truck maybe. Or at the least, it looked like one of those vans in the last scene just before someone goes missing—forever.

But it was your mobility for a while, your line to the real world, and maybe even peace of mind. We could get you and your electric wheelchair back and forth to doctor appointments and elsewhere.

We eventually sold it and came out somewhere near flush in the deal, according to my less than astute mathematical capabilities.

But the main reason I mention the van is a single incident—one eventful night. It wasn't "dark and stormy" as so many stories start.

We were returning from ZZ's restaurant, one of the few in our small town. It was the first place you wanted to go upon your return home, and bless the staff and customers, they gave you an ovation when you wheeled in. I wish I had a mental image of what your face looked like, but I came in behind you. I do have a photo from the evening. It is of you and friends Sam and Jeb Banks, who happened to be there when we arrived.

A first public appearance after so long a stay is a big deal, but most of Brownsville had come to see you in the hospital. And besides, The Event of the evening was yet to surface.

It occurred later on that return home, just me and you, with your mom driving her vehicle.

You had asked me in the hospital if I thought you could get back to the mound before your senior year became a dusty old annual.

Now, I have never been a believer in telling you or any other child what they can't do regarding their goals.

I follow the "Listen to the Mustn'ts" Shel Silverstein credo. It's a poem I often read to you as a child.

"Listen to the Mustn'ts, child. Listen to the Don'ts.
Listen to the Shouldn'ts, the Impossibles, the Won'ts.
Listen to the Never Haves, then listen close to me.
Anything can happen, child. Anything can be."

God bless the late Silverstein for instilling possibility in the imaginations of children, you among them.

Also from the school of Silverstein, I was not about to tell you what you could not do.

I kept it real, though, and told you the pitching could likely be done, but the healing and strengthening of that injured leg was the biggest hurdle.

Nothing was mentioned of added complications, of learning how to catch and throw with one arm while on one good leg, all in less than six months.

Now, remember me, the doubting Taylor, if not Thomas. I also mumbled something about maybe—through hard work, healing, and time—you could get back for an opportunity with some of the smaller colleges and maybe it could happen . . .

It's funny. A select few especially stubborn souls just refuse to put maybe on their life's menu. They don't serve it. They don't eat it.

My friend Brandon Rowland, mentioned elsewhere in this collection, is one. Landon Wilson is another.

Also, did you know the word "maybe" can sometimes unleash a force of nature? I must admit having never personally experienced the rumbling of a volcano ready to blow. But on that night, driving around the old high school, I was as close as I ever will be.

Oh, there was no lightning bolt from the blue like in Robert Redford's *The Natural.* But something fabled, fast, and furious was going down in the atmosphere in that ice cream van (that just happened to have a wheelchair lift). Now, I write all this on the other side of the famed story, but again, it was a soul-charged, so-shall-it-be-said-so-shall-it-be-done moment.

The atmosphere changed. I could feel it.

I looked at your face way back there in the rearview mirror. Cast in grill-like shadows from the upright wheelchair ramp, and I swear some sort of beacons most folks call eyes shot lights outward.

"THERE'S NO WAY IN HELL I AM NOT GOING TO BE BACK ON THE MOUND FOR MY SENIOR YEAR!" your voice echoed in the ice cream van.

Honestly, old doubting Taylor, dad, or Thomas was gutpunched. Maybe I am not as much of a negative Norman or doubting Thomas as I am a Roger realist. I thought first of your disappointment. Honestly, my heart sank when you said it with such van-rattling words laced so with will, hellfire, and damn-the-torpedoes.

I was tired of seeing your hurt.

But little did I know, right? It was a proclamation. A turning point. The point in the story where the hero picks a path.

You were beginning your climb. And though we kept it for a couple of months, the white van was one of the first things you left behind on your ascent to the mound.

Sir Winston Churchill is credited with saying, "A kite flies highest when it flies against the wind, not with it." It was not long until you abandoned the wheelchair as well as the ensuing walker that needed an extension to match your height. I think you grew an inch in the hospital.

Inch by inch, you were climbing. Willpower is a peculiar thing, and in my Roger-realist opinion, it is a miracle when it's also God's will.

Photo by Oscar Esquivias

Landon Wilson needed eight surgeries during a forty-day-plus stay in the hospital. His left arm was amputated. A rod was inserted in his right leg, which was severed to the bone. Screws were put in both ankles, but he climbed back atop the mound.

"Getting to the top of any given mountain was considered much less important than how one got there: prestige was earned by tackling the most unforgiving routes with minimal equipment, in the boldest style imaginable."

Jon Krakauer, *Into Thin Air*

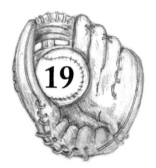

Seeds of Faith Grow

OK, I'll admit it. Mending a mangled body, undergoing eight surgeries, and learning to pitch with one arm and one bad leg in less than six months may not seem all that hard for some to believe. To a few, it may seem quite the miracle, especially to those so close to the story. Or maybe to you, Landon, it's just another day in the life. But I will tell you that you did an incredible job of keeping your comeback from me.

When I think about it, this may be the most farfetched part of it all. I was aware you wanted to play again, but I knew little about the reality of your actual return to the mound until the first day you pitched again.

Sure, I knew you were back at school and even going to rehab with Torry Patrick, physical therapist and program manager at Sports Plus Rehab Center in Brownsville. But in the back of a mostly empty mind, I thought, "The kid is trying to get back in the real world—the day-to-day living, not playing baseball."

Heck, I didn't even know you were trying to pitch again, until my friend and then high school basketball coach Kendall Dancy sent me a video clip and a text saying: "Have you seen this!?! Amazing!"

It was a clip of you pitching and catching in the high school gym.

I had intentionally taken a big step back from baseball. Because I was the famed doubting Thomas, and more appropriately a realist Roger, I did it to protect myself, maybe.

There is no doubt as a parent, I wanted to protect you. It's a natural thing to do, and sometimes not necessarily the right thing to do. I was already considering that any mission back to the mound was likely to end in a dose of failure, disappointment, and heartache. Maybe my step back from baseball was me insulating my heart and soul from that result. Maybe I hoped to be already calloused when this same realization finally entered the head of an eighteen-year-old. Was I already lining up a Plan B in the event of failure?

Regardless, surrender wasn't in your search engine. Stubborn, however, would be atop any Google search one conducted for Landon Wilson.

In fact, one of your one-time classmates and my former student, Mattie Ford, sent us a letter in the hospital. She has known you since you both were grade-schoolers.

Landon is hard-headed and stubborn, Mattie pointed out. What some may see as a flaw was what was going to help you get through your ordeal. "He doesn't give up on what he believes," she wrote.

It was a student-becomes-the-teacher moment for me. I remain so glad she took the time to send us that spot-on observation.

Those who succeed, who face overwhelming odds, who eventually own and grasp their goals—those people like you don't worry about failure or the fall. They really are stubborn to a fault or maybe even blissfully ignorant to the risk.

And again, as Guy and Susan Clark wrote: "He did not know he could not fly, so he did."

So few who are afraid of failure succeed.

Even with the realization, "Hey, he is really going to give this a shot," your mom and I never expected it to be the third game of the season, in early April. It was a not no, but hell-no moment ... that became hell yeah!

There we were, riding to your senior season's away game number three. We get a call from you on the bus: "Hey, can I pitch today?" SEE THIS BLANK SPACE RIGHT HERE >_____< ?

That is the time warp that my head went into with that question.

I will never know how you talked your coach into allowing you to pitch so soon. (See words above, where Mattie Ford called you persistently stubborn.)

I remember your mom and I discussing it, mostly in disbelief, and evidently the conclusion was it was now or never, Elvis.

Everest's peak was in sight. And climbers will tell you that leg of the journey can be the most precarious. It's thin air there. Hard to breathe and helicopters don't fly well. So many things can and do go wrong, they call it the Death Zone.

But your mom-and-pop ground crew gave the go-ahead to move forward. Talk about a gamble and so many things that could go wrong. Ah, life is nothing but a step for a stepper, and you wear size fifteen cleats (really).

We get there, and sure enough, there you are warming up. The cycle of surreal had circled back around.

I took a photo of you. It's as forged in my heart and soul as is the first time I held you and shared our first words, "I've been waiting on you."

By the way, on your first birthday, your hair was red like your mom's, and it still tints red in the light. My mom had made that call long years before you arrived on planet Earth, and it came to pass long after she left. Mom told Beth and me, "One day, you two will give me a redheaded boy."

So yep, you're really a member of Team Ginger—redheads with their stereotypical passion. Is their *fiery* label fact or fiction?

I don't know, but you seemed to be carrying an intense torch atop that practice mound.

Walking alongside the fence, I watched you warm up. I stopped and took a photo, which I would later emblazon with Matthew 17:20: "Truly I tell you . . . If you have faith, you can say to this mountain, 'Move from here to there'; and it will move. Nothing will be impossible for you."

And truly I say to you, Landon. I still look at it as a daily reminder to me, just another sinner trying to find his way safely home. Your successful climb embedded this lesson in my life, every day. And when I get the chance, I pass it on.

Do you think that is too much of a dad thing? Or is it a Christian thing? "Oh, just in case you don't believe in the power of prayer . . ." I might start off when I show folks the photo or a film clip of you pitching back then.

But back to your return. Say hey, Wilson, if not Willie, THERE YOU WERE, AND ON THE MOUND.

So many stars had to line up so you could see this peak. So many things seemingly wrong had to be corrected. And it was so a fish-or-cut-bait moment, a play-ball, get-in-the-game moment. There was no turning back.

I was nervous. The unsinkable Beth Wilson may have been nervous, but if she showed it, I couldn't tell.

Now it may be the baseball dad in me, but I also think there was some electricity in the air. I know it was for me. People there who knew, knew.

The announcer for the game walked up to me and asked if I would give him some information about you. I said sure and went into the press box and looked at the blank notepad and pen. In front of me, the room's elevated window framed you on the mound.

And there this scribe was, with a loss for words. Tears formed and edged the corners of my eyes. Like a reporter past deadline, I fought to come up with something. I had twenty-six letters to put in some sort of order that would describe a miracle.

Yeah. Yeah. Of course, "Do you believe in miracles?" came to mind. It's that incredibly famous call by sportscaster Al Michaels while watching the USA hockey team win the gold in 1980. To say I didn't hear that in my head would be a lie. Thanks, Mr. Michaels.

But there you were. Atop your Everest, and though I wasn't at the peak with you, your mother and I were on the support crew a few hundred feet below.

By the way, it really is hard to breathe or think up there in thin air.

I can't remember exactly what I wrote. Maybe it went: "...Landon Wilson returns to the mound today after being hit by a car while training for baseball. He spent nearly fifty days in the hospital. He endured eight surgeries and worked incredibly hard to get back to the pitcher's mound today. Please welcome him back."

Now as then, I am still stunned to write something as simple as that. The reality was nearly overwhelming. Emotions banged around inside my body like a racquetball. I went into the restroom, and a few tears streaked my face.

A friend came in, looked at me, and said, "Are you all right?"

"Yeah, I think so ..." I replied, knowing I might never be all right.

I don't remember much about the game. My pregame advice had been: "Get you some pitches in. Get some outs. And get the hell out of the game!"

I think the final score of the game was 3-2, them. When you came out of the game, we were winning (2-0, maybe?).

Our friend, attorney Michael Banks, told me he later announced to a Brownsville board meeting, "Landon Wilson pitched today." Applause followed.

Is that an only-in-a-small-town moment or what?

Sure, but it's a heck of a moment, showcasing why we should be grateful we live in such a small town.

Team Wilson went home with hope that night. A storm was beginning to pass, but we had to learn how to survive the rest of the season on the top of a mound that is a mountain.

Photo by Morgan Timms

Landon walks back to the bus with head coach Tyler Newman after a district win.

"You've got to jump off cliffs all the time
and build your wings on the way down."

Ray Bradbury

Our Secret

Dear Landon,

I knew a secret.

How's that for a hook to keep you reading?

The deal here, though, Landon, is you knew it, too.

There we were at the orthopedic surgeon's office. And we talked about when you should get back atop the mound.

And the surgeon concluded, "Well, I still think you need a little more time before you get back on the field."

You looked at me; I looked at you.

We shared one of those unspoken, yet intensely communicated father-son moments. DNA is weird.

Did we smile? Did we wink? Did I have the look of fear or the look of pride in my eyes? Both? Were your eyes glowing with a secret joy, like having taken an undetected chocolate chip from the jar?

Yeah, we both knew you had already pitched several games.

OK, here's where I hear the other readers' questions. "How

could a parent in their right mind do that?" someone out there has already asked themselves.

Well, I have already mentioned the famed cheese not being far from sliding off my cracker; or, as Waylon Jennings sang, "I've always been crazy, but it's kept me from going insane."

What's my best defense for allowing you to play so early? Again, it was a race against time, and I was battling a willpower that had become a force of nature.

"We are all told we can no longer play the game," is the *Moneyball* quote used elsewhere in these letters. And there is also the famed saying, "There is no time clock in baseball." Well, you were on one.

Your parents did this—proceed without at least one of your surgeons' knowledge—because we wanted you to fly again, even at the risk of a costly fall. The scheduled flight was limited to an exceedingly small window of opportunity.

I had already toted the heartbreak of letting you choose to go running that night. Personally, I was willing to gamble against a second tragedy so that I could fend off the heartbreak of the first.

And, too, there's falling, and then there's falling while trying. You, your mom, and I are of the latter conviction. DNA is potent.

To clarify: Technically, according to one medical expert, you weren't supposed to be back on that mound.

Actually, your leg had not grown back together yet. The accident had claimed a portion of your bone and left a space that needed to mend. And that other ankle had screws in it.

Ah, but no one told the engine that it couldn't be done. We hadn't asked, either. The reality was this engine and his crew didn't or wouldn't hear it. Heck, the engine was already on the hill.

* * *

So many stars aligned for you to return to the baseball field. Things fell into a divine order. Don't forget to be grateful.

Among this alignment was the fact you had a coach who wanted you back on the mound as much as we did. Without his green light, without Coach Tyler Newman putting you in the lineup, you'd have never thrown another pitch in a high school game.

And yes, he gave his endorsement only after talking to us. If something had gone wrong, it was still all on your mom and me. And, of course, I'd go as far as to put it all on me. If something happened, I would have to bear the burden. I had already agreed to let you take that run on a dangerous road that night.

Watching your warmup, what you told me when I asked how you would defend line drives came to mind: "You know I've been hit by worse, right?"

Coach Newman was on the team to get you back to playing. And at the root of it, despite the nature of a coach, he knew the challenge was about way more than wins or losses.

It says a lot about the man.

I hope when you are old like me, you send him a thank-you note. Ah, heck, why not send it right now?

Photo courtesy of Haywood High School

Returning to school was exciting and included a very warm welcome and a police escort for Landon.

"No, I cannot forget where it is that I come from
I cannot forget the people who love me
Yeah, I can be myself here in this small town
And people let me be just what I want to be . . ."

John Mellencamp, "Small Town"

This, Too, Shall Pass

Dear Landon,

I mention prayer often in my letters to you. Perhaps it's because what we went through made me need and believe in it more. Maybe I'm hoping you will want and need it, too.

Prayers were said for you before, during, and after your ordeal. These messages to God sprouted and flourished all over, but our small town really had a megaphone and possibly a satellite.

This thought of collective prayer reminds me of when my old friend Jake Waddell reached out to me at the hospital and made me laugh when I so needed it.

"I have never seen a small town come together like this in prayer. I'm glad, 'cause the devil is a son of a biscuit eater, and he's working overtime."

Now, Jake didn't really say "son of a biscuit eater." He said something else, and that's likely what made me laugh most.

Like me, but better at it, Jake is a self-professed sinner trying daily to follow the Word.

He was right about our town coming together in prayer.

Some might say social media is what made the congregating-for-a-cause so possible and obvious. I am not sure about that, but I have seen it happen again and again in our town since your ordeal.

I have often made the quip, "I'm from Brownsville. It says 'a good place to live' on the water tower. We would have put 'great,' but we didn't want folks to think we were bragging."

True, small-town living can be a blessing and curse. It's good in that everybody knows everybody, and it can be bad because everybody knows everybody. For example, everybody knows your business (might be deemed bad), but if you have a flat on the side of the road, somebody's likely to stop and help, because everybody knows you (good).

And let's be honest, not only do we know everybody in our small town, heck, most of us are also related. Is there danger in a shallow gene pool?

Seriously, the people and the famed "place where we come from" wrapped a lot of love and prayers around us in a troublesome time.

You would go down to all your surgeries with a prayer blanket made by hometown ladies who cared.

You would arrive home with a wheelchair ramp already constructed by men who worked and prayed together.

When you first went back to school, you had a police escort complete with flashing lights. Several of the first responders in that procession had also been on hand the night you were injured.

Small town, yes, but oh so very big at heart.

* * *

And oh, yeah, here's an added note stemming from that same conversation with Jake.

He and I talked about the saying, "This, too, shall pass."

Most folks say it when times are bad, and that's applicable, but never forget it can also apply when times are good. As with small-town life, there can be two sides.

The equal and alternate meaning that so many fail to see is that good times are fleeting. When things are going well, also remember the good times, too, shall pass.

One legend has the phrase coined by King Solomon as words that would apply to all situations.

The saying is even represented by three Hebrew symbols: the gimel, zayin, and yodh. Some folks sport it as a tattoo, but I think I'll just keep it in my head. I don't have anything I want to wear every day, except maybe a Cardinals cap.

The gist of "this, too, shall pass" is something I've mentioned to you before. We can only live in the now. Time marches on. Everything shall pass.

> *"...And if, and if the night runs over*
> *And if the day won't last*
> *And if your way should falter*
> *Along the stony pass*
> *It's just a moment, this time will pass."*

U2, "Stuck in a Moment You Can't Get Out Of"

Photos by Taylor Wilson
Hunting buddies for life. Landon, Sam Banks, and Bond Lonon
hunt at Open Lake in Lauderdale County, Tennessee.

"I was a hunter from the time I could walk."
Wilson Rawls, *Where the Red Fern Grows*

Return to the Wild

Dear Landon,

Getting back on the mound was just one of many goals you had while lying in that hospital bed.

Driving was one. Creatively, we would wheel your electric wheelchair alongside your vehicle, and you slid into the seat.

"Don't tell your mother," I remember warning. You drove around the house a few times and we soon tested the waters on the road. And, of course, the floodgates opened.

Someone called me: "So and so just swore they saw Landon driving through town."

Like driving, returning to the outdoors was another goal.

I really did carry you hunting with me as soon as you could walk, and you loved it.

Fishing, of course, with better weather and more action to keep a youngster occupied, was what we did most in the early years. We often went after school.

Admittedly, we also sometimes went hunting and fishing before school.

I remember amid some sort of bird flu (crows and jays were carriers, they said) I dropped you off at pre-K after a morning dove hunt. Yeah, you were wearing a few feathers, some mud and blood, but you promised not to tell your mom. I guess the teachers understood.

The urge to return to the hunt is primal in my book. And honestly, fishing is really hunting, too. One is searching/hunting to capture something. Volumes have been written on the hunt, the primal psychology of it, the graduation through the ranks of what it means: from killer, to numbers, to challenges and trophies, and finally ending up as someone who simply enjoys being out there.

William Faulkner hinted at the complexities and ironies of hunting in a short story, "The Bear." It's the part where he writes about hunters having a love for what they must kill.

There is great irony in it.

The older you get, the better you will understand what we're really hunting for most often includes a good time among friends and hopefully more than a limit of fine memories.

Our friend Steve "Gofer" Darnaby helped get you back to duck and deer hunting. Darnaby may very well have introduced more kids to hunting and fishing than the Hatchie River bottom has mosquitoes. His love for the outdoors cannot be denied, and his excitement for it is infectious.

Hopefully, like so many of my friends with whom I surrounded you while growing up, his influence will always remain.

I'll never forget a silent morning, in opening-day darkness. We were loading the boat to go duck hunting, and you could not be there due to your injuries.

Out of nowhere, overcome with emotion, Darnaby admitted the difficulty of you not being with us as had been the norm for years.

Tearful glances were shared among us all. It was hard to handle, a silent moment, with another opening-day sun about to show.

It was a stark reminder that life goes on, and hopefully we all spend some time realizing how much we care for others and enjoying their company.

One goal upon your release from the hospital was a successful deer hunt. I rode shotgun with you and Darnaby on that adventure.

"I hope one steps out right there and goes, 'Oh $%&!,' " Darnaby said.

And what do you know? That's what happened. The deer stepped out, as if on cue. It stood there, seemingly wide-eyed at its error, and you dispatched it.

Oh, there was another celebration of a goal met, a step climbed.

You know there are celebrations, and then there are celebrations with Gofer. Again, as down to earth as God can make a man, Gofer is an awesome sponsor, counselor, confidant, and friend.

Was there any better deer jerky than the one that one provided? I don't think so.

Of course, the major objective among all outdoor-geared goals was returning to the duck blind. Now a duck blind is really a camouflaged clubhouse of sorts, a remnant of most childhoods.

Waterfowling has long been your favorite, and you so wanted to get back in the club.

No irony was wasted on me that the place you most wanted to return was called "The Right-Hand Arm," a Mississippi River river-run off Open Lake in West Tennessee. We have hunted "The Arm" with Billy Lonon and his boys Bond and Walt since you were all old enough to tag along. You shot your first duck, a green-winged teal, there with a youth-model 20 gauge. Borrowed from Brandon Rowland, it was the same one I had watched Brandon use to shoot ducks.

You and Billy went out and chased it down.

Thanks to Team Lonon, we got you back there, too. It's a magical place and a magical sport.

There you first began realizing the need for tools as an amputee. "Do you think I can somehow use a broomstick to help me hold the gun?" you asked.

You were also able to go on a late-season hunt with Billy's relatives Trey and Ware Lonon near the Hatchie National Wildlife Refuge.

A post-hunt photo of that day has Darnaby's grandson, Clayton Pinner, in it. He is wearing a "Landon Strong" shirt in support.

The following fall, I went with Darnaby and Clayton on the youngster's first squirrel hunt. Within weeks, the boy would be diagnosed with cancer, and he and his family would successfully wage a larger-than-life battle against the disease. Their fight would go twice through the trenches of treatment and would last close to two years. Their battlefield was primarily St. Jude Children's Research Hospital in Memphis, not far from where you fought yours.

You ordered several "Clayton Strong" shirts. I so admired you for that. But his family would go with "Pinner Strong," which made more sense because Clayton's dad, David, was also battling cancer. But I still wear my "Clayton Strong" shirt, a collector's item no doubt, as a reminder of those with hearts like lions.

Clayton and you are survivors. You've stormed the front lines against impossible odds and won.

Landon, I know you don't believe it, but when you're near forty and Clayton's around thirty, it will seem like you are closer to the same age. Time is funny like that.

I hope you can somehow get together and exchange notes, battle scars, and memories of surviving your respective struggles.

And who knows, perhaps you can spin a hunting yarn about Gofer, the Lonons, and maybe even me.

Many helped you return to the outdoors. They know the call of the wild and understand your love for it because they love it, too.

Photo by Taylor Wilson

Three years after their first trip, Landon joined up with Bill Dance again for a return fishing trip.

"But man is not made for defeat ..."
Santiago, *The Old Man and the Sea*

A Fish Tale

Dear Landon,

When you were in the hospital, you got a ton of care packages, cards, and more. One came from the famed angler Bill Dance, his family, and staff.

We can honestly never repay their kindness.

Bill even put you on his social media platforms, and more messages of prayers and concerns arrived in the mail or electronically from all over the nation.

Having known and written for Bill for a few decades, I was not surprised he reached out. He is truly one of those people who means it when they say, "If there is anything I can do to help, let me know."

He is also a prankster, a people person extraordinaire, a wonderful storyteller, and an educator. No one has taught more people to fish than Bill Dance. I went to see him get an honorary doctorate degree from the University of Tennessee. The degree was in fisheries and wildlife, but it could just as easily have been awarded in education.

It was a longtime goal of mine to see him get that deserving honor, and I finally got to check it off my bucket list.

Weeks before your accident, we fished with Bill on the Mississippi River in the shadow of downtown Memphis, where you would spend so many days in the hospital district.

I lined it up and called it your senior trip. Your friend Tillman McRae went with us. As you have always noted, few have the athletic ability of Tillman. "But all he really cares about is hunting and fishing," you'd laugh and add. There are worse things to care about, of course.

Those who have not seen Memphis from the Mississippi River have missed something. It's a wonderfully unique view of a city that, for many rural West Tennesseans, is basically our Oz. It's where we would go, especially in the pre-Amazon days, when we need something big. I guess all communities have their fabled Emerald City, somewhere off in the distance. But one thing we know about Oz: One must go through trials and tribulations before its magic can help you find your way home.

That day with Bill on the Big Muddy in Memphis was one in the sun, but dark clouds loomed. We had no inkling that a few blocks away stood a building complex of untold horror—and help.

Would we have enjoyed that moment more if we'd known we were about to go down a dark road?

Flash forward a couple of years, after the major trials surrounding your injury. Bill would again take time to do one of the things he does best: Take someone fishing and teach them about it.

You had not fished since the accident. In fact, the last time you had fished was the Big River trip with Bill. A return trip meant something more.

The outing was primarily scheduled because Brandon Boyd, your fraternity brother at Mississippi State University and an excellent bass angler, also wanted the chance to fish with Bill. Who doesn't, right? I know Brandon appreciated the opportunity.

Now, I hate to ask Bill for favors, and whenever I have, it has never been for me, always someone else. And this time, I guess the favor was for Brandon, or so it seemed at the time. And, well, I found it very honorable that you wanted to do something for a friend. Loyalty ranks up there with courage in my book.

Anyway, we were going fishing, and the night before I spent a couple of hours rigging up ways for you to hold a rod via boards, rod holders, etc. But never mind all that, the next day you were in the classroom of Dr. Bill Dance. He quickly taught you how to land fish again, minus an arm.

Laughter was heavy in the air as you and Brandon caught many catfish. Bill worked that magic, like he always does. He tied fishing and fun into a knot we'd never forget.

For that day, all was right. The storm surrounding your accident had *o-fish-ially* passed. But, of course, as veterans of dark and dangerous storms, we know there are always more on the horizon.

Did you enjoy this return trip more because of the accident—because we now had knowledge that bad things can happen anytime?

I did. As an old man, I also know that good days are limited, few, and far between.

In Ernest Hemingway's *The Old Man and the Sea*, his main character and angler, Santiago, has a continued string of bad luck. He even loses his trophy marlin to sharks. But Santiago refuses to label his trials bad luck. His is a story of the refusal to admit defeat, marked with the notion that willpower and effort are more important than results.

Luck is irrelevant when people work together.

How many people worked to help you bounce back from your injury?

In the end, Santiago brings home a trophy like no other, but it is ravaged by predators. The trophy has no real value, but the story does. It gives him integrity and a bit of legacy like Ted Williams's wish: "When I walk down the street, people say, 'There goes the greatest hitter that ever lived.'"

Like Williams, Santiago and his tale about a big game fish would live for years in his village.

When you are an old man like me, what will people say when you walk down the street? Knowing you, I doubt you care. My good guess at your quote is: "I don't give a $%&!"

But at the end of *Old Man*, despite Life's *luck* and predator sharks, the old angler reunites with a youngster whom Santiago taught to fish, and they plan to fish again.

I like that, always: the plans to fish again. Always consider those plans, will you? And who knows, it may be with Bill Dance.

Photo by Taylor Wilson

Landon's dad found new understanding of the difficulties people with disabilities face after shoveling the ramp to get Landon into the building for the high school play.

"You've gotta have heart . . ."

Damn Yankees, musical, "Heart"

All the World's a Stage

Dear Landon,

Another goal of yours while in the hospital was to return home and perform in the annual high school play, which, appropriately enough, was *High School Musical.*

A snafu in administration did not allow a school play your eleventh-grade year. But it was on again for your final year, and you wanted to be on board.

A lead role was center target, but how was that going to happen? There was not enough time, and honestly, at that point you were lying on your back with something akin to an Erector Set wrapped around your leg. Who knew if you could make it back to that stage, much less a pitcher's mound?

Thankfully, Emily Carpenter took the reins of the play that year (bless her heart). She came and visited you in the hospital, and very aptly found just the right part for you and your circumstances.

It snowed a lot during rehearsals. We had to figure out how

to get you and your heavy electric wheelchair into the building. I was routinely becoming much more aware of the daily battles of the disabled when I stood at the bottom and looked up the long, snowy, old-school ramp to the theater. I tried but just couldn't get you and that electronic chair to the top entrance.

Fortunately, former student and football player extraordinaire Decourtney Reed came along and helped.

I taught nearly all the Reed boys. Great kids. And I can still remember once asking where Decourtney was, as the middle school baseball bus was about to leave. Then the band happened to march by and Decourtney was leading it, banging on a big bass drum, in ball uniform and barefoot. I got him on the bus, but he forgot his cleats and was known for a while, by me, as Shoeless Decourtney Reed. Among my memories of the play-rehearsal days, he will always be Back-Saver Reed. Not only did he save my back; he had our backs.

While you rehearsed, I went home and got a shovel, returned, and cleared off that ramp from top to bottom.

Mrs. Carpenter said something about how much your dad must love you. If she only knew. If you only knew. (Maybe you will see it in a Glove Letter.)

The play was a success.

You were back on your feet by showtime and did extremely well. Your part called for you to basically be a DJ. It also made me realize that if you wanted, you could easily go into broadcasting. Lord knows, broadcasting must pay more than teaching.

In the opening of the play, you and boyhood buddy Brandon Evans did the crowd greeting. Showing the exits, you pointed to the left and right. Brandon stood behind you and seamlessly became your left arm, pointing to the exit.

You came up with the joke. Since it was the first time some in the audience had seen you since the accident, I could feel a bit of hesitancy, maybe a touch of uneasiness, but they laughed. It was good stuff and well played.

Later, while at Mississippi State University, you would attend a fraternity costume party as Monty Python's famed Black Knight from *Monty Python and the Holy Grail*. I know your brothers likely put you up to it. But dang, the guts to do it—that says a lot.

Also, this was around Halloween and the anniversary of your injury, and I was at home moping and feeling sorry for myself. Then I realized, "Hell, I got this kid who's walking into a party, likely shouting, 'TIS NOTHING BUT A SCRATCH! Why in the world should I be depressed? I should be celebrating, too."

You have never shown much concern over being the amputee (most often the only one) in the room. I did find it interesting once that you told me you like rooms with mirrors, so you could watch people who were looking at you.

I really think both your experience on the stage and standing out there on the pitcher's mound have given you a degree of confidence some are missing.

Getting back on that *High School Musical* stage was about rejoining your friends, but I think it was also your way of proclaiming: I'm back!

By the way, Brandon also brought you a Christmas shirt when you were in the hospital. On it was a gingerbread man whose arm had fallen off, and it said, "Oh, Snap!"

We all laughed.

Team Wilson considered wearing one for our Christmas card that year, just the family photo, with no explanation. It would have been great. But we never did; there were too many doctors' appointments and other Landon Wilson goals to pursue.

But thank God you made it back to the stage, and for friends who believe in you, have your back, and especially for those who can laugh with you in the most trying times.

Photo by Taylor Wilson

Landon's story earned Sports Story of the Year honors in the *Jackson Sun*.

"Storytelling is the essential human activity.
The harder the situation, the more essential it is."

Tim O'Brien

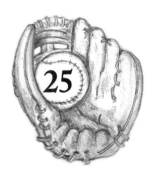

The Tale You'll Tell

Dear Landon,

The season wore on. I don't have actual stats, but they are probably out there somewhere.

I don't think you lost a game your senior year. Regardless, rest assured you had a winning record in more ways than one.

I can't remember how many games you pitched in, and my recollection may be clouded. However, selective recall or not, you never came out of a game in which you started pitching with a losing score on the scoreboard. That most likely makes you loss-less.

And even if someone accuses me of being a baseball dad, I still don't imagine my numbers are far off. So those wanting to disagree, well, they can kiss my seat cushion.

I don't know how many strikeouts you recorded, but there were more than one might expect. Your disability forced you to think more how to create outs. You had that talent with two arms. The skill, and need for it, only magnified when you lost a limb.

You pitched several complete games, and most of several more. You won some district games. You won a postseason playoff game, and you even went 2-3 at the plate in that one.

At season's end, you collected several team, district, and regional honors for sheer heart and courage. You also made the All-District Academic team and the West Tennessee All-Star Team.

You were no stranger to awards. Before you were hurt, you had won All-District, All-District Tournament, and All-Academic awards your sophomore and junior seasons.

The perseverance and success for your last season also earned *Jackson Sun* Sports Story of the Year honors for 2018.

I am also proud that in this edition of the paper, the athletes chosen in the number two and three stories are also from your high school. This includes football player Taylor Shields, whose dad, Patrick, stopped a gunman at a football game, and Jamirah Shutes, who scored a record number of points in a state basketball tournament.

I had the privilege of teaching all of you, and I am proud of that, too, and keep the edition framed on the wall at school.

You batted five times on the year. All efforts were late in the season, as your body was healing.

Is that the right number of ABs? If I am wrong again and people call me on it, well, likewise kiss the seat cushion. My mind's eye says you batted four times in tournament play and once in the West Tennessee All-Star Game. That would be two for five. That's .400, and for one arm, a bad leg, and just learning to hit again, hey, not bad.

But it was your pitching experience that aligned with God's will and enabled you to return to the field. If you had not been familiar with pitching, getting back on the field wasn't going to happen your senior year. Center stage was the only place for you to fit. I suspect, given more time, you could have adequately played first base again.

And your one-armed hitting skills were returning when you called it quits. That would later prove of value when you took up golf.

Did you pitch against the toughest teams on the schedule?

No.

That's baseball. The game should always be played to win. Your coach made decisions he needed to make. And with my recollection of you being undefeated on the mound, it seems his coaching choices were good.

But as for the season's ending honors—true recognition, trophies, plaques, and other such hardware are nice, and I hope you are grateful for them.

I have several for sports and several for my work as a journalist. All are still appreciated but also collecting dust. Someday, you will likely have to throw all that away. Don't feel bad about it. Heck, maybe I'll get rid of them myself.

When the last out is made, it's not the metallic-covered hardware that's relevant. What matters most is the story you carry with you.

A good question might be, "Does your personal narrative inspire and marvel at all the magical stuff that can surround the famed human experience?"

If the answer is yes, you carry a distinction with you always.

"There is no such thing as coincidence;
it is God winking down upon you."

Unknown

An Inspiring Godwink?

Dear Landon,

Three out of your four years in high school ball, your team fell one game short of going to the state tournament.

I missed those final playoff games for two years straight because I was with your grandfather, who was suffering from cancer.

Your team was one game away from going to the state tournament your junior and senior years.

With a lot on the line in your final playoff game, understandably, the one-armed pitcher wasn't going to pitch. So I didn't miss your playing time by being with my dad, which I would have done regardless. Still, I heard you put on a performance.

From the dugout, some shreds of DNA of my aforementioned curse, the Taylor temper, showed up in you. You argued ball and strike calls with the umpire, and he threw you out of the dugout. Since you weren't in the game, where else could he toss you?

The tale you told me was upon being tossed, you threw down

your prosthetic and walked off. In full-tilt Taylor tantrum, I can only imagine what you said. I think that was the only time in hundreds of games that you got thrown out of one.

Now, in my mind I understand the frustration. It was your last game, and you were not on the field. You were, as they say, "being told it was your last time to play the children's game." You didn't know you would get to play in the year-ending West Tennessee All-Star Game at the time.

"I figured I might as well go down in flames. You know, make a memorable exit," you told me.

And hey, maybe the calls did favor the home team. We've all seen that before. It's baseball.

But of most interest to me was the postgame story you also told me. You said that as you stood away from the field, cast out, still fuming, and watching the perceived end of it all, a girl who had also lost her arm came up. She said she was aware of your story and just wanted to mention that you had been an inspiration to her.

"Well, I am not being a very good role model right now," you told her.

I wish you two had spoken at a time when your mind was clearer and calmer. Through word of mouth and similarities of your stories, I was vaguely familiar with this young lady. It seems she was an achiever, too.

Now that was a small, interesting occurrence to old Dad. Was there a reason for her to be there at that place in time to simply offer you a word of encouragement at that trying time?

Now, I've long been a believer in the magic of the right word at the right time. I teach and live by it. Mark Twain said the difference between the right word and the almost right word is the difference between the lightning bolt and the lightning bug.

And likewise, with me being an everything-has-a-reason guy, you know what I think.

Sometimes God really does wink.

Again, connections are peculiar, and so are the linked reminders of what's important. We just need to recognize these cues/winks.

I have no doubt that God does it because it's simpler than, "Hey! Over here! Don't forget the meaning of all this! And, by the way, it's bigger than a ball field."

It also tends to make us think. Or maybe He just wants to laugh and say, "Gotcha!"

Following your senior year, your team would finally get to the state tournament for the first time in school history. A talented team, they lost two straight in the tourney.

The ensuing spring was lost to COVID-19, and oh, how I pained for that season's seniors, having lost a season of playing time, whatever the sport.

Can you imagine having a pandemic take away your senior season? Think about that. If the pandemic had occurred in your senior year, there'd be no opportunity for you to climb back atop that mound.

Timing really is everything, cliché or not.

Satchel Paige was heralded as Major League Baseball's oldest rookie (reported to be anywhere from thirty-nine to forty-two) when he began pitching for Cleveland. A quote machine that might make Mark Twain envious, Paige said, "Don't look back, something may be gaining on you."

But I'm looking back in these letters, anyway, and I have been amazed time after time—a lot of things lined up for you to accomplish your goals.

Landon throws out the first pitch at a minor league game with the AA Mississippi Braves.

Skip: "You guys, you lollygag the ball around the infield.
You lollygag your way down to first. You lollygag in and out
of the dugout. You know what that makes you? Larry?"

Larry: "Lollygaggers."

Bull Durham

A Minor (League) Note

Dear Landon,

Your last game was the West Tennessee All-Star Game at what was once called Pringles Park, a.k.a. "The Big Chip." That's where the Southern League AA minor league teams played in nearby Jackson, Tennessee, under various names and for various MLB affiliations.

We Wilsons are familiar with what's now called The Ballpark at Jackson, via our friend Mark Beason of Jackson, Mississippi. Mark is one of several people who helped you choose to attend Mississippi State University. For years, he has also been a part-time employee and host family for the AA Mississippi Braves, an Atlanta affiliate.

Because of the shared love for The Game, Mark often hooked you and your friends up with tickets when the AA Braves came to AA Jackson. Back in those days, we'd load up in a second and go

to the park, especially with a fist full of free tickets. We came to
know many minor leaguers through Mark and would go see them
at Pringles when they came to town.

That was a big deal for you as a kid, and I hope your childhood
memories will always be laced with those moments.

After your recovery, Mark added another good memory. He
arranged for you to go down and throw out the first pitch for a
Mississippi Braves game.

That one pitch? It was in the dirt but catchable by a semipro
catcher. After the game, you showed me the ball with the dirt mark
still on it. "I almost blew it," you laughed.

When you were younger, we also went with Mark to the AA
Southern League All-Star Game in Huntsville, Alabama, and to
the AAA Braves game in Gwinnett, Georgia.

(Wrestler Ric Flair was there that night. WOOOO! Sorry, I
couldn't help it.)

When you were injured, several players you had met sent you
messages of concern and inspiration.

Kala Ka'aihue and friends sent you a get-well message and
photo from a golf course in Hawaii with all displaying a shaka
sign. (Many Californians call it the hang-loose sign.) Hawaiian
lore says the shaka originated from a sugar mill worker who lost the
three middle fingers on his right hand. Switched to guarding the
train, he would hold up that hand to show all was clear. Children
began mimicking it, and it is now recognized around the world
as the Hawaiian way to symbolize friendship, understanding,
compassion, and solidarity. Talk about a bad thing transforming
into something good.

Former minor leaguer Willie Cabrera sent a thumbs-up photo,
an inspirational note, and a Bible verse from his home in Los
Angeles, California.

The verse was Proverbs 3:5-6: "Trust in the Lord with all thine heart; and lean not unto thine own understanding. In all thy ways acknowledge Him, and He shall direct thy paths."

I think you learned a lot from the minor league acquaintances. For one thing, you learned how hard it is to make it to the majors.

Kala earned Southern League MVP honors. Willie played on a high school team from which, I believe, five or six of its players signed to play professional ball. Most of the minor leaguers you met were incredibly talented but did not make it to The Show. They were by no means lollygaggers as famously mentioned in *Bull Durham*.

Only one of the players we met would make it to the bigs. It was utility player and Pennsylvania native Phil Gosselin. He would go on to play for the Braves, Diamondbacks, Pirates, Rangers, Reds, Phillies, and Angels. His longevity in the league speaks volumes for versatility.

We celebrated Gosselin's debut by watching on TV.

"That's so weird, we were just eating hamburgers with that guy last week at Steak and Shake," you said.

Lesson learned? Dreams can come true.

Want another lesson?

OK, I remember once we were eating lunch near the ballpark at Bass Pro Shops in Pearl, Mississippi (basically a suburb of Jackson, Mississippi). You asked Kala if he had time to give you some hitting tips. You'd brought your bat.

Kala said something like, "I'd like to, Landon, but I have to leave here and go to the field, train, run, have team meeting, get taped up, then get on the field, warm up, batting practice, play the game, and then the postgame stuff."

"WOW! That sounds like a job!" you said.

I pointed out that it was. We all laughed.

I didn't point out until later that Kala also did that same routine nearly every day, for most of the year, and for little pay, all in pursuit of a dream.

Lesson learned? Chasing your dream is hard work.

I think the meal money per player was $20 a day back then. Kala was big enough to have had football scholarship offers.

"Do you know how far $20 goes with me?" he laughed.

Good host families are godsends to minor league kids.

So, Mr. Mark, as you called him, and all his connections doled out a lot of kindness to you, sent you south to ring a Mississippi State cowbell, and added to a love of The Game that stretched from Jackson, Tennessee, to Jackson, Mississippi, and everywhere else.

He also searched for, found, and mailed you a baseball signed by Pete Gray. The famed one-armed outfielder played for the St. Louis Browns in 1945. Gray likewise was a minor leaguer in Memphis for the Chicks. He lost his arm above his elbow in a childhood accident. Not to insult Gray, but I do want you to note here: Gray had way more than five months to learn to play with one arm.

Landon Wilson and grandfather Lloyd C. 'Butch' Wilson celebrate after the West Tennessee All-Star Game in Jackson, Tennessee.

"But all endings are really beginnings.
We just don't know it at the time."

Mitch Albom, *The Five People You Meet in Heaven*

The Last Game

Dear Landon,

As noted in a prior letter, you played for the final time in the West Tennessee All-Star Game at what was Pringles Park in Jackson, Tennessee.

Every pitcher got to throw one inning. Before you tossed yours, I noticed you speaking with the umpire. After the game, you told me that he was the umpire who called your last game, also in Jackson, Tennessee, but with your Batters Box club team.

The same umpire who called your last game with two arms also called the last game you tossed having only one.

Life is so strange and cyclic.

In the game, each roster's pitcher was allowed to throw one inning. Yours was scoreless, thanks largely to a great throw from an outfielder for the third out, which I think was made at second.

Three of your high school teammates—Tillman McRae, Kylan Shaw, and Brent Moore—also played in the game. I coached/

taught all of you when you were kids and remain proud (and relieved) that you were somehow able to overcome my coaching.

Tillman made a crazy play at shortstop early in the game and earned defensive honors. Kylan got a hit (doubled or tripled, maybe?) for the other team. It was one of the few hits their team had, and it earned him an award for offense.

The team you and Tillman were on won with a lopsided score.

In addition to pitching your scoreless inning, you also made a trip to the plate.

"I think the coach thought I was joking when I said, 'Can I take a cut?'" you laughed after the game.

And I'll be damned if your hard-hit ball, going perfectly into the 5.5 hole, wasn't snagged because the defense was trying to cover a base runner. You made an awkward run to first, though. You even tipped your helmet to the crowd. No one but members of Team Wilson knew your leg had yet to grow back together.

After that, I was relatively certain you were out of The Game for good. I finally sat down. It was beside our friend Chase McLean, a Jackson Christian School coach who had provided you pitching instruction when you were younger.

We talked a little about your season, about the fight to get back. This game was a fitting end for a new beginning.

Weeks later, there was some interest and talk of you playing college baseball somewhere small.

But I remember an almost defiant response, when you simply said, "Hey, I don't want to go anywhere and be someone's mascot! If I go, I am going to play."

I know what you meant, and the reality of getting that leg back in shape to play competitive college baseball was a challenge you did not undertake. In fact, as of this writing, you still await a surgery on it.

That all-star game was likely a much better way to go out. It was certainly better than ending it with that playoff game where you got tossed like your old man.

And by that time, your grandfather had gotten back enough strength to come see you play at Pringles.

I am so grateful he got to see your last game. I took a most valued and memorable photo of you two afterward. Smiles all around. He is in his wheelchair; you are sporting a prosthetic that brandished black tattoos.

Oh, I can easily see the image, even now. Two warriors, both having overwhelmed what life hurled at them.

Of course, later your grandfather would pass away and finally go safely Home. I bet he ran across Heaven's plate. Or maybe he went in with a head-first slide.

And as you know, I have likened him to a Tom T. Hall lyric, in that old dogs and children loved him. But he was also a rough and tough football player, too, a high-school All-State, and nominated for All-American. He loved sports, but he had a special affection for baseball. He was a Cardinals fan who passed this passion, and the art of batting left-handed, along to both of us.

He loved you much, as he was fond of saying.

Another photo, one of the big, one-armed kid reclaiming that mountain, was always near his bed.

He lost his own dad as a child, his mom to cancer when he was in high school, and his first wife and high school sweetheart in his early forties. He suffered for several years through the pain of cancer. He was bound to an electric wheelchair and eventually bedridden.

Finally, there was just a great soul imprisoned in a worn-out shell. But long before he took that final turn at third and headed for Home, he told me with faith-filled and steely eyes that remind me of yours when they blaze: "Taylor, Landon is going to be all right. I've been through a lot, and it always works out."

When I look at that picture of you two, I know he was right.

Photo by Taylor Wilson
The Wilsons' Wiffle ball field—affectionately nicknamed MoonPie Park after the cheap snacks served there—once sported its own Green Monster wall in homage to the famed wall at Boston's Fenway Park.

"Ah, but I was so much older then; I am younger than that now."

Bob Dylan

Diamonds Are Forever

Dear Landon,

I didn't hear the if-you-build-it voice, but you and your friends (Preston Evans was one) suggested we build a Wiffle ball field in our backyard when you were young. And like Ray Kinsella in *Field of Dreams*, I was crazy enough to listen.

Built on a teacher's budget, its first rendition had a tall left-field wall made of synthetic flooring I had torn up and replaced in our home. After nailing it up, I painted the wall Boston's Green Monster green with a ninety-nine-cent can of spray paint. One-time volleyball net posts served as foul poles. Since spray paint was cheap, we coated them the appropriate Hi-Viz, foul-pole yellow. Dog kennel panels were the backstop, webbed plastic fencing was held up by zip ties, and PVC pipes rounded it out. The field grew to be a magic place on weekends, where Wiffle balls and spirits soared.

We served Tennessee-made MoonPies, because they were inexpensive treats, and labeled it all encompassing MoonPie Park.

I have long wanted a giant MoonPie logo to put somewhere along the fence.

Ages from three to sixty-plus have played the children's game on that patch of ground. It's not as magic as the Field of Dreams . . . but there's some mojo, for sure.

MoonPie Park went away for several years after your accident. I'll never forget the day I took it down. "Life changes," I tried to explain to myself, with much more than an inkling of hurt every time I mowed over what was.

But hope runs rampant in the hearts of geezers like me. And, as mentioned elsewhere, life is about circles. We round the sun; we round the bases. Life makes its way back, especially to reminders of what was once good and can be good again, says fictional author Terrance Mann in the *Field of Dreams* film.

MoonPie Park returned, with little prodding and a mere mustard seed of thought strangely familiar to the Blues Brothers' line, "We're getting the band back together."

Selfishly, I had plans to extend the pond over the area (again, less mowing).

But the field resurfaced with you in college and home for the summer. Evidently, I take requests. The old man (me) brought it back, with the same ingredients: kennel panels, PVC posts, plastic fence webbing, and zip ties. Your mom helped with the financing, but she drew the red financial restraint line at buying lights. I do have the utility poles on the trailer as I type, though. Between you and me, hope springs eternal for that, too. Right field was designed with a shallow porch. The old man bats left-handed; so do you, but with one right hand.

Build something good and people really are drawn to it. Take a Wiffle ball as an example. Scour the search engines for how much advertising the company has put into their product. The answer is: next to none. As a book about the northeastern company notes, the product has remained successful with little to no advertising or product placement. The yellow plastic bat and white ball with eight slotted holes are now Americana.

So MoonPie Park proved if you built it twice, they will also come back.

You and your buds played many a game that first summer. I was stunned at how much faster and quicker you'd all become in contrast to me, with an aging body that's obviously going the other direction in the skills department.

Still, I feel young teeter-tottering about MoonPie Park, relegated to mostly ground crew now—watching, having a cold beverage, and making snide remarks.

Maybe y'all tolerate the old man being around because he was the one who re-released the magic.

There's a Chuck Clark quote about three-fourths of the world being water, and it being an indication the Lord really intends for us to be fishing. At the least, it's a good excuse to go.

Well, think about this. A Wiffle ball has eight slots. There are seven days in the week. So eight slots could mean we are supposed to play Wiffle ball seven days a week and twice on Sunday.

My logic lost you, right?

What I'm just saying is, if you get a chance to play the children's game, at age three or sixty-three, do it. Build the field, or at the least buy a plastic ball and bat.

And oh, Landon, there's a real world out there. It's where you no longer play the kids' game (or at least not as seriously). But take heart, once baseball's chalk lines are drawn on your heart and soul, you find ways to be near The Game. Some of those ways might even involve zip ties and dog kennel panels.

MoonPie Park has been around enough, forged enough memories, to stir the soul in a few generations. It's kind of like Doc "Moonlight" Graham said in *Field of Dreams:* "Once a place touches you like this, the wind never blows so cold again. You feel for it, like it was your child."

Oh yeah, I am a pawn for the mystic.

Your dad, who believed in the Easter bunny and Santa way longer than he should, is prone to flights of fancy well beyond Hi-Viz yellow foul poles. In my defense, big bunny and the North Pole resident brought me shotgun shells in winter and fishing tackle in spring.

I like to imagine MoonPie Park connects you, me, and everyone who's played there. And heck, if nothing else, maybe it has made for some charmed feel-good memories.

Baseball, or some semblance of it like Wiffle ball, can always make you feel young. It can also take you back to a time when magic is for real.

Son, don't neglect the potential that baseball can always be so much more than a game.

There's a beauty and truth to it, and yeah, I know the ad slogan is soccer is the beautiful game, but also bear in mind the origin of soccer is most likely Roman soldiers kicking the heads of the vanquished around. And hey, the sound of that mental image certainly doesn't sound nearly as beautiful as a round wooden bat squarely connecting with a leather-wrapped sphere.

WHACK!

But to be fair, maybe all games we loved as kids have such mojo. Still, between us Wilsons, well, it will always be baseball.

And sure, the Real World is going to march in and sometimes trample over us, and maybe even back up and do it again. But remember you can always find fragments of magic out there in select realms, like in a game played on a diamond.

Does baseball's allure or wonder ever fade among those most afflicted? Nah, I just think Life gets in its famed busy mode, and it becomes more difficult to see and enjoy.

I mentioned *Field of Dreams'* Doc "Moonlight" Graham a couple of times in my letters.

This is the same Doc who had a blip of an appearance in the majors and went on to become a physician in the real world. In the movie, the same doctor left the magical field to save a child's life.

In the movie, Ray also realizes Doc's wisp of a pro ball career and mentions how coming that close to a dream would be a tragedy to most.

Doc famously replies, "Son, if I'd only gotten to be a doctor for five minutes . . . now that would be a tragedy."

So we step out into the real world and do what we must to survive. We abandon the field to provide for our families and maybe, now and then, try to make those places outside the foul lines magic, too. Or at the very least, we try to make them more tolerable, enjoyable, kind, and "better."

In the back of our mind, though, we keep and cultivate those fields of dreams. And if we're lucky, we can go back there, sometimes via a bleacher-creature seat at Busch in St. Louis, and sometimes via a yellow plastic bat and some white plastic spheres.

Holy cow! All that makes me long for a beer and a hotdog, or maybe better, a yard chair and a MoonPie.

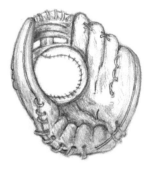

Epilogue

Dear Landon,

I t seems like ages since you were injured.

The memories of what happened to you can still be painful now and then, but as time has gone by, the game we played together has transformed into something larger. It's become much more of a win than a loss.

Maybe that's easier to consider since we now know how so much of it turns out.

I have even heard you reflect, "All that time in the hospital wasn't entirely bad. I do have some good memories of it."

It really wasn't all bad/sad. We gained a stronger faith because of what happened, and we all know to take nothing for granted.

And I don't know if I told you, but your incredible attitude made that trip through a near tragedy easier on your parents. I hope the amazing mindset you displayed through your trials will always be with you, and you can call upon it should you need it again.

I can promise you that life will always be challenging.

I don't live a day without counting my blessings to have you.

When you see the need, try to encourage others with your story and what you achieved. Let people know miracles happen, and do not hesitate to pray.

I have long said of the accident: "I was just so glad my son was alive, and that I could hold him and talk to him. I could care less if he is missing an arm. To me your brave heart is what makes you my son, and obviously you have one. Continue with courage."

Second Timothy 1:7 says, "For the Spirit God gave us does not make us timid, but gives us power, love, and self-discipline."

My wish is for you to be happy and for you to strive to do the right thing. Help others as so many helped you. Give God thanks for the opportunity to still be riding around the sun on this round ball we call Earth.

I love you much,

—Mom

About the Author

Taylor Wilson comes from a long line of storytellers, educators, and farmers.

"Many of my folks were all about growing things, be it in the fields, hearts, or minds. So my DNA has me getting up every day and trying to continue their tradition," Wilson said.

For much of his career, Wilson was a reporter, managing editor, freelance writer, and photographer, who has written for newspapers, magazines, and websites. He now teaches English and creative writing at Covington High School, in Covington, Tennessee.

Always a baseball fan, Wilson claims he can still, even as an old man, pitch an increasingly less commendable game of Wiffle ball.

Lightning Source UK Ltd.
Milton Keynes UK
UKHW020640161121
394011UK00007B/496